Love Affair in the Garden of Milton

LOVE AFFAIR

IN THE

GARDEN

OF

MILTON

Loss, Poetry, and
the Meaning of Unbelief

SUSANNAH B. MINTZ

LOUISIANA STATE UNIVERSITY PRESS

BATON ROUGE

Published by Louisiana State University Press
www.lsupress.org

LSU Press Paperback Original

Designer: Michelle A. Neustrom
Typeface: MillerText

"Fullness of Time" appeared, slightly revised, in *Sonora Review* (Fall 2018). "Into the
World before Us" was a semifinalist for the 2019 *River Teeth* nonfiction prize. "Paper
Cranes" appeared, in different form, in *Cagibi* (October 2019) and was shortlisted for
the 2019 *Cagibi* Macaron Prize. "Wild Work" is reproduced from *Prairie Schooner* 94,
no. 4 (Winter 2020), copyright 2020 by the University of Nebraska Press.

Cover photo by Omar Alejandro on Unsplash

Library of Congress Cataloging-in-Publication Data

Names: Mintz, Susannah B., author.
Title: Love affair in the garden of Milton : loss, poetry, and the meaning of unbelief /
    Susannah B. Mintz.
Description: Baton Rouge : Louisiana State University Press, [2021] | Includes
    bibliographical references.
Identifiers: LCCN 2021001335 (print) | LCCN 2021001336 (ebook) |
    ISBN 978-0-8071-7581-1 (paperback) | ISBN 978-0-8071-7639-9 (pdf) |
    ISBN 978-0-8071-7640-5 (epub)
Subjects: LCSH: Mintz, Susannah B. | College teachers—United States—Biography. |
    Milton, John, 1608–1674—Influence. | Adultery—Psychological aspects.
Classification: LCC LA2317.M527 L68 2021 (print) | LCC LA2317.M527 (ebook) |
    DDC 378.1/2092 [B]—dc23
LC record available at https://lccn.loc.gov/2021001335
LC ebook record available at https://lccn.loc.gov/2021001336

CONTENTS

PREFACE

THE SQUARE YELLOW clock on my desk is chugging along the minutes. At each rotation of the golden second hand, it makes a gurgling sound like it's clearing its throat, then there's a click and a brief pause as second and minute hands cross. I'm about to turn fifty-five, and I've had this clock since before I was ten. It's practically a relic. Its top is cracked, the alarm is bust, and it long ago lost the clear plastic insert that protected its face. But it's never stopped telling me the time, and it never runs slow. I learned how to meditate using this clock, back when it was new, and I refer to it now, pulling it away from the wall and turning it toward the chair where I sit across the room. I'm trying to revive my practice, quiet the noise in my head, find some space of stillness.

Last month, at the start of December, I went to a five-day silent meditation retreat, the longest stretch of intensive meditating I'd ever done. The irony of marking my experience with meditation by my ancient timepiece, whether across the years or in any given session, isn't just that mindfulness trains us to attend only to the present as a way of fostering composure for life's challenges. It's that I can't get away from the past. One of the fundamental principles of mindfulness—maybe the hardest for me to grasp, obsessed as I am with time and inclined by temperament and education to analyze anything to within an inch of survival—is that getting caught up in the stories we tell about ourselves, comforting as they feel, can trap us in a ferocious repetitiveness. I like opening my eyes to that little yellow cube of my own continuity, but I'm also trying to let her go, the girl whose fears and shames I've been rehearsing for a lifetime. Especially now, heading toward the last third of a life, unexpectedly single. Except, not quite.

At the retreat, one of the instructors described her devotion to mindfulness as a love affair. She was speaking of the refuge of meditation. I had gotten myself to this retreat after many years of longing to achieve a profound calm, and in that moment I wanted to trust that I, too, could cultivate an equanimity so dependable that it would feel as good as love. But later, writing secretly in my journal (we were encouraged to avoid journaling as a distracting entanglement with our habits of mind), I considered that "love affairs are always fraught." Wasn't it a love affair, after all, that had ruined my marriage? Isn't any love affair, if not an actual fiction, wildly complicated, built on fantasy, subject to the fluctuations of desire, and practically guaranteed to end? The very words connote the illicit, the short-lived, even the sordid—certainly not a forty-year relationship with Buddhism.

Then I wondered if such contradictions were the point. Some affairs do last a long time. They aren't *inevitably* forbidden. No relationship can sustain a high pitch of excitement, just as mindfulness teaches us to abide neutrality without restlessness. Any involvement will eventually grow mundane. Something will invariably go wrong. Loved ones get on our nerves, demand our patience and our forgiveness. Love is work, but paradoxically, it tends to go best when we stop trying so hard to make it right. In mindfulness, too, we try to witness rather than strive, to accept what is instead of obsessing over perfection. Maybe it goes without saying that I knew *about* mindfulness more than I was practicing it around the time my husband started his own affair.

It's impressive to declare you're in love with anything other than another human being, since it implies an unexpected intensity of emotion, and such pleasure, such joy. When we remember all the rest of what love really is, the humdrum everyday quality of most of our experience, a love affair with mindfulness makes sense. I spent my first day at the retreat catapulting between craving and agony. Every part of my body screamed in pain, and my mind pinged scattershot in a hundred directions. I could not get quiet. Then I could not forgive myself for failing at the thing I'd been wanting to do for such a long time. Then I could not relieve myself of disappointment that I was berating myself (again) for not living up to my own expectations. A thudding and all-too-familiar troika of critique. It wasn't until the third day (or more accurately, something like the thirtieth session of meditation in thirty-six hours) that I discovered the tranquility I was hoping for, an expanse of it opening before me. Then I had to remember that hoping for it to recur would defeat the very state of nonreactive witnessing that meditation hones in us. I had to remember not to beat myself up for falling into that particularly Western, goal-oriented trap, and then to be kinder to the part of myself that isn't kind to myself. Stillness was available beneath all that spiraling self-talk once I calmed the whole system down. I don't yet get the *feeling* of a love affair with neutrality, but that's the idea of mindfulness as refuge: a whole plain of neutral experience that's quite rejuvenating, once we stop oscillating between elation and gloom.

The love affair that rent my marriage apart didn't precisely end my marriage. We're legally separated, have lived apart for years, but we're not divorced. Grappling with that ambiguity is one endeavor of this book: what it means to be stuck, to carry on in conditions that defy category. At the same time, why does anyone—why do I—care, as long as it's working? Just the other day a neighbor asked what happens to my dog when I go on vacation, and I told an unnecessary lie ("He stays with a friend . . .") because I couldn't get my mouth around "ex-husband"—not because he is and I'm ashamed of that, but because he isn't, and in my literal way I want the proper nomenclature. I've had to adjust to the ongoingness of a limbo it's in my power to end, except that I can't decide that I want to. And limbo, too—that liminal holding space for the spiritually unassigned—is entirely the wrong term to describe a couple of atheists orbiting their failed marriage with gravitational pull. Behind the daily vacillations, the screeds against his wrongdoing I sometimes orate aloud and the defensive insistence that loving relationships can take all forms, lies a deeper motivation, to set the heartbreak of separation in the context of mindfulness. Trauma had initiated a frantic search for meaning, for restoration, but experience is never that neat. We might feel encouraged to wander more freely if we truly believed we were tough enough to handle whatever arose.

It's this concept of meandering to arrive at your proper destination that brings my story to the garden of Milton. I was teaching Milton the first semester after I separated from my husband, and it's only a slight exaggeration to say that that experience saved me from a worse despair. There's a currency to Milton's work that resonates, not just for a scholar like me but for anyone sunk low and searching. Anyone whose life has gone off the plot—*upheaved*, as Milton would say, by turmoil and the loss of hope. Where do we turn for consolation, for repair, when a certain future disappears and our sense of the past becomes a convoluted entanglement of untruths? When the stories of ourselves, the comforting, well-worn narrative of *who I am*, no longer hold true, and if religion holds no explanatory truths?

It's common to think of Milton as a Christian, if also revolutionary, poet whose major work trains our attention on the mistakes of hubris and overreaching as well as the "happy end," the promise of the good to come after so much destruction and trespass. But the title of *Paradise Lost* misleads us, purposely so, and cleverly, if you consider that the point is to rethink what goal we have in mind when we're judged (or judge ourselves) for having strayed. What have we *really* lost if we're kicked out of a place that wasn't all that fulfilling to begin with? What satisfaction can come, unexpectedly, of hard work and renewed understanding between two people who've failed each other so spectacularly? When we reorient ourselves to *this* life, rather than the presumed magnificent afterward, what good can we do now? That's one of Milton's most radical implications: if we eschew notions of an afterlife altogether, everything is at stake only in this moment. If we can rest with discomfort, with ambiguity, with the terror of life's elusiveness, maybe we find a more rewarding joy. If we quit our habits of framing, explaining, and containing, get out of our own way, maybe we allow ourselves to be more authentically astonished.

Milton had three wives, and lived through civil war, and wrote poetry much further into the future than even he, with his epic aspirations, could have imagined. He defended divorce, lambasted compulsory piety, limned a revolutionary Eve. His work demands that we think for ourselves, at the perilous intersections of every moment of every day. It's dramatic, and exciting, and alive. That's what I clung to in the ghastly unreality of shock, of a beloved becoming entirely *strange,* and a sadness that threw all the old frameworks into disarray, when the forward motion of my life yanked to a halt: Milton's endless, ornate sentences, his lush poetic lines, his electrifying clarity of purpose. *Paradise Lost,* but also Milton's divorce tracts, his political tracts, his drama *Samson Agonistes,* all figure here as guides for how to think about the world turning upside down. Because it will. We can try to reconstruct ourselves in the aftermath of chaos, according to what we know, or we can unlearn ourselves completely, open to the possibility of otherwise. That was the extraordinary discovery of an otherwise lamentable autumn: *all the world before me, where to choose.*

Here, then, is a tale of how we might elude the constraints of story. A tale about longing to believe, when you have no faith in a god. About the trauma of infidelity, when the absence of belief seems to deepen the reeling, disorienting pain of betrayal. About the lyric intensity of grief, and the saving grace of verse—especially Milton's world-bending heresies and humanist convictions—when nothing else seems to cohere. About teaching, even when you're rocked, a teacher of thirty years, by a crisis of irrelevance. About dogs, friendship, conversation, travel, mindfulness, aging, choice, and happiness, all as forms of devotion to what Milton himself would cling to, late in his career, as ballast in the face of failed revolutionary zeal: learning how to live to the utmost of your know-how. And, too, about accepting that the best life just might mystify all our certitudes and effort. Just the other night I dreamt that my wedding dress was stained with ink, a black smudge that bloomed to purple and yellow and green as soon as I touched it with water.

WE ARE SENSE-MAKING creatures. But when my marriage collapsed one August afternoon, and nothing made any sense at all, the whole enterprise of figuring things out seemed both frantic and utterly useless. Painfully *unfamiliar.* Why did he do it? Even he couldn't say. What would I do now? No one could tell me for sure. How would I survive the disruption, live toward an unrecognizable future, reclaim an identity outside of the one I'd been crafting as part of a couple? It's not that I lacked for answers. There's hardly a song with lyrics ever written that doesn't purport to tell you how to react to heartbreak.

And that ubiquity does offer some solace. So *this* is what it feels like, I'd think for many months after that summer's instant of revelation—this is the rupture of an affair, of a marriage coming undone—and whatever cavalier notions I'd ever had about all that, the commonality of divorce, flew out the window. The actual windows of the house I owned, to which he had done so much renovating work that it resembled the structure I bought ten years prior only in the barest of outlines. Banal in its ordinariness, the story of an affair, and yet devastating, a form of disappointment whose aftershocks surprise us for years.

The end of a relationship has no social rituals to ease its burden: no recognized expressions of sympathy, no mourning costumes or colors, no devoted section of greeting cards. No strict period of bereavement or funeral, no cloth thrown over the mirrors or candles set sail upon a sacred river. More often than not, in fact, it is inflected by accusation and guilt, with friends rallying around to stoke your anger more than honor your grief. The ceremonies of death, whatever we believe about ushering the departed toward an afterlife, primarily aid the living. We are reminded of the communities we inhabit, reassured of our place in the larger social networks in which we have designated responsibilities. Taking our place in these roles can ease the sense of bottomlessness that follows a great loss. Death rituals corral the chaos of grieving, give us something concrete and limited to do, distract us in the near term from a future that now looms with frightening vagueness. The memorializing solidifies us again, when we might have felt ourselves disappearing into weightlessness. It signifies that we, too, are loved. But the end of a relationship has no such dignifying formality.

In fact we assume that a couple that splits has not been happy. What's the point of being sad about that? And yet a breakup *is* a demise of sorts, and we might well mourn it like a death. Maybe the separation has happened so suddenly that we lose our balance utterly in the wake of it. I often felt that I was defending my right to mourn the loss of a man who had hurt me. Early that fall, a friend announced that I would no longer be "in crisis" by the start of the new year. How could she possibly know? When another implied doubt about why I wasn't rushing toward divorce, I tried to explain the dizziness of the about-face. Just weeks before, I'd been in love with my husband, planning the next decades of our life together. It wasn't I who flipped the switch. How—or maybe why—was I supposed to obliterate all that?

In the immediate aftermath, life carried on in alarmingly regular fashion, aside from the animal howls that came rasping from my throat at night and the fact that I spent most of my time lying down, when I wasn't propelling myself into breathless sprints around my block, desperate to quell the sense of physiological alarm. But I did not suffer dissociative fugues. My hair did not turn white overnight. I did not smash my husband's belongings, throw his clothes into the street, take up drinking at noon, stop bathing, go immediately to bed with someone else, or recover from loss to start my second chapter in a storied love in the south of France. I wished for that kind of dramatic release, for a visible sign that something unprecedented had happened. Everything was different, and yet so much of it looked, I think, from the outside, confusingly the same.

Inside I was searching, madly and vainly. We learn the structure of storytelling not just from our earliest afternoons in nursery school but also from the basic impulse to account for the constant bombardment of experience. We pose questions relentlessly, ever more profound as we grow up, many simply unanswerable, interrogating this life of pyrotechnic complexity. The very asking justifies the systems of thought that evolve to relieve the pressures of our curiosity and our fear. Olga Tokarczuk writes in her haunting novel of nature settling a score that "we draw maps of meanings for ourselves . . . [a]nd then we spend our whole lives struggling with what we have invented" (223). My bafflement produced not a paucity but a surplus of answers, because we're so good at coming up with them. Explanation is reassuring; it is "cozy," as the Buddhist teacher Chögyam Trungpa would tell us. But getting "caught up" in story, in another common mindfulness phrase, even if it temporarily quells the chaos, can box us into unforgiving emotional states and have the effect of making us less rather than more resilient. That obnoxious roommate who lives in your mind, the one who might look like you and never shuts up, can be very persuasive. But at some point, if you start to listen in to that nonstop nattering rather than losing yourself in its soothing rhythms and familiarity, maybe you recognize its less useful dimensions, its helpless repetitiveness, its delimiting lack of creativity.

Of course it's not easy, breaking habits of a lifetime, and we have to grasp a counterintuitive truth that striving so hard for respite rarely leads to a lasting sense of ease. Even harder to trust, maybe, is the idea that obstacles *are* the path, rather than a deviation from it. But that's what Milton's Eve implies to Adam at the end of *Paradise Lost*, telling him, on the brink of expulsion, "Lead on . . . in me is no delay." She can have no illusions about the road ahead. Or more accurately, she's never experienced anything like what's about to happen to her, bad or good, beyond the perimeter of her life to date. Still she's eager to venture forth into that unknown. She's had to unlearn a few false stories of identity along the way, but she's also had practice, too, in Milton's surprisingly existential Eden, figuring out how to live by her own lights, secure in the strengths within her.

Love Affair in the Garden of Milton

1

FULLNESS OF TIME

WHEN THE DOG went missing and then was found, it did not make sense as a random event. He'd never run off before—that's why I let him wander the halls of my workplace, untethered, to call on his friends, human and canine, like an old woman in the midcentury South, or a European *flâneur*. He was the epitome of good behavior, the very *apotheosis* of it. But that day, something unintelligible occurred, some impulse or spark that I could not understand but that he pursued, out of the building and into the woods, where snow was on the ground and the temperature that night would dip toward zero. That he was rescued, four days later, running for the life of him toward home, along a busy byway, still wearing the blue-and-red argyle sweater I'd put him in on that Wednesday, now soaking wet but with no other sign of wear, wonky knees pumping him north, seemed nothing short of miraculous.

Over the days, weeks that followed, as the story took hold, this was its pith: the two frigidly cold days, worst of the winter, followed by six inches of snow, followed by a morning of wet rain—we'd always begin with the weather. The dozens of friends and strangers who came out to search. My estranged husband who drove fifty-two hours from LA to New York when I emailed to say, *Jack is missing, this is that emergency you said you'd come back for,* the two of us tracking an Etch A Sketch of paw prints across campus where students were studying for finals. One woman showed up with her electric grill when we decided, because a stranger had texted me so, that the smell of cooking bacon was a sure-fire trap for terriers. I had never fully appreciated the expression "it takes a village"; then I walked up to a man I'd never seen before slogging through snow with a big black Lab, in search of a dog he didn't know was mine. *This isn't how it ends,* I would think, *the story of Jack,* not after everything that had happened. It would have made no sense.

I might have gone out of my mind, speaking of nonsensicalness, had I been able to feel at all through the elusive sightings and near-misses and maddening phone calls at dawn from someone who'd just spotted him running toward the dorms or chapel. Emails and posts to the Facebook page one of my sisters made to "Help Find Jack" numbered in the hundreds; people clamored for updates; I was writing the story as it happened, and that was a way of embedding meaning into something that felt intolerable, because I didn't think I could stand one more loss. My husband and I had been separated for over a year; we adopted the dog together; words like *lost* and *missing* were freighted with history. Meanwhile there was freezing to death and starving to death and getting hit by a car or eaten by a stoat. And then, on the fifth day, two cars going in opposite directions converged on a little dog in a blue-and-red sweater. Someone slammed on the brakes. Someone stopped traffic. Someone yelled at her husband to *get that dog!* Two men ran into the trees in knee-deep snow; a sweater snagged on a fence; one of them emerged minutes later with Jack bundled up in his coat. I didn't know him either.

There were lessons to be learned in all of this, about community and perseverance and help, to say nothing of knowing, as now I do, how to get a frightened dog to approach you when the 99 percent of his DNA that is wolf has reverted to the wild. Wild instinct saved him, surely; is it also what made him run? I don't understand why he did it, and I don't understand how he lived. His tracks were spotted miles apart. He weighs ten pounds; it was the dead of winter. Then he was in my arms again, wrapped in a blanket, without a scratch. Alien abduction seemed as likely as anything. What I do know is how strong the impulse is to make something of this story—to make this *into* story. You say miracle, I say the intrepid grit of dog, we're both putting a spin on the thing.

* * *

WHEN MILTON'S EVE wakes up in the Garden of Eden, her first impulse is to follow "a murmuring sound / Of waters" to a pool that seems to her "Pure as the expanse of heaven" (4.453–54, 456). Full of wonder about where and what she is, she bends down to look, and what she sees in the water determines everything that happens next, from the poise and grace of her bearing to the revolutionary act of eating the apple. A face appears "within the watery gleam" that seems "another sky" (461, 459); Eve is taken aback, it's taken aback, and then both faces lean toward each other "with answering looks / Of sympathy and love" (464–65). In that instant Eve is her own mother, conferring the gaze of recognition upon her infant; she is an infant discovering a face in a mirror she doesn't know is her own. She is a lover returning her beloved's validating regard, and a woman who, in her very first moments of awareness, turns to the world in a spirit of profound reciprocity. She sees sympathy and love in the pool because that's what she brings to it.

For years scholars read this gesture as the poet's not-so-subtle way of rendering incipient narcissism in his first-of-women (he was well-versed in classical myth, after all), but I think it's Milton at his proto-psychoanalytical wisest, anticipating by centuries the theory that the grooves of selfhood are laid down in our earliest experiences of attachment. The poem makes it clear that Eve's curiosity is less about *who* she is than *where* she is. "I . . . found myself reposed," she says (450), emerging into self-consciousness and inclined to figure things out for herself rather than to cry out (as Adam later does) for instruction or companionship. Eve's problem isn't sinful self-regard; it's that she comes into a world ill-equipped to manage a woman so content to be alone because she finds creative potential everywhere. The story of paradise is not about being expelled from it but about trusting others to be there when you come home, even if, say, you suddenly go walkabout—which is what Eve effectively does in book 9, walking off to garden alone because she believes (just like her poet-creator) that without being tested we are never truly free.

I am far from alone in reading Milton's Eve as magisterial in her courage, a self-sufficient woman whose relationship to all things heavenly is one of bristling annoyance at constantly being pulled away from the pursuits that please her and defined in terms of roles, as helpmeet to Adam and mother to mankind. Of course Eve would eventually have tired of an image with whom she couldn't fully connect; equivalence is not the same as reciprocity (to say nothing of the importance of touch in any affective bond). Her truest pleasure through most of the poem comes from tending the garden, because *paradise* is a milieu best defined as doing what one does, an intersubjective space in which creatures of all kinds simply are themselves, and find ways of responding to each other without debt or coercion. I wasn't thinking about John Milton when Jack the dog wandered off one day, but I'll admit that like a petulant Adam I did take it personally. His bolting seemed so *purposeful*, a rebuke perhaps of how much I had come to depend on him, those alert black eyes trained on me, that profound animal intelligence at my side all the days and nights of being suddenly no longer or not-quite married, an anguish I had never felt before.

Yet I know that his leaving had nothing to do with me (can I say the same of my husband?), and that his survival was pure self-determination. You tuck your tail over your nose and find a place to burrow against the cold. This is how I choose to understand it, that 99 percent of your DNA knows exactly how to handle the situation when you look up and think, *shit*, how did I get here? The trick is trusting your imaginative instincts.

WHEN I REALLY fell in love with *Paradise Lost* (if you discount the massive transferential crush I had on the man teaching it), it was writing about the gorgeous lyric intensity of book 7, which recounts the creation of the world. If there's one book in the epic that sounds positively intoxicated with its own poetic exuberance, it's this one, where an unfettered use of language has mountains "upheav[ing]" into the sky (7.286), a "tawny lion, pawing" to free himself from "grassy clods" (463–64), elephants throwing "earth above them" as they "upheav[e] / [their] vastness" out of the ground (468, 471–72), birds "ruptur[ing] forth" from eggs (419), and seas "swarm[ing]" with "fry innumerable" (400). What book 7 performs for us is a mind so completely immersed in its medium that it seems temporarily to have forgotten what it's supposed to be writing about, which is another way of saying that despite the patently human core of *Paradise Lost,* this account of animal, vegetal, mineral *aliveness* may be the best poetry of the poem.

We might wonder what has captivated the author's attention so totally as to distract his intellectual purpose, except that would be entirely wrong, because the lesson of book 7 is that what Adam ruefully refers to as Eve's "strange / Desire of wandering" (9.1135–36) is precisely how we find our way to truth, which Milton describes elsewhere as the scattered body of Osiris. *Everything* wanders in Milton's ethical universe, and there's nothing wrong with deviating from the straightaway if you do so with considered intentions—which makes the point of all the biotic brio of creation, with its emphasis on arriving into existence knowing just what to do, a model of existential integrity. It's not about getting *there* but about being *here,* in Milton's world, occupying with unexpectedly Buddhist mindfulness an environment that abounds with creatures happily occupied in doing just what it is that they do.

This kaleidoscopic nature, chock-full of self-sufficient beings also deeply attuned to each other, forms a vital philosophical backdrop to the human story of Adam and Eve. Milton understood that to achieve the fullest self-expression, we need the emotional resilience to be able to *play.* The psychology of his work is suffused with acts of reaching toward the object-world for what might transform us ("she pluck'd," he writes of Eve, and "she ate" [9.781]). That is the rich dialectic of self-experiencing. We pursue a sound, a smell—call it scent of ripe apples, or squirrel! (if you're a dog)—wherever curiosity takes us, and we find ourselves in that unknown, altered and renewed. This is why contentment is rendered, in the final moments of the epic, as a state of being wholly at peace with oneself *as is.*

WHEN JACK CAME back, and I could safely ponder what it had all meant—when I could turn off the flashlight and try to imagine him sniffing his way atop a crust of snow in pitch-black woods, without my heart stopping—when I could lean *into* meaning instead of guarding myself against the threat of grief, I felt only bafflement. I'd let out the lead and watch him script a baroque curlicue from one side of the road to the other, ueys and figure-eights and punctuation marks of pee. But it spelled nothing I could read. So wondrous was his return unscathed that to deny a spiritual dimension in the whole escapade just seemed churlish, and at least one friend who knows of my unbelief insisted that my faith in Jack proved I have a soulful side. I think it's a question of framing. Did Jack get lost *so that* I would learn something I needed to know? There was a moment one night, home alone and numbed on Xanax and whiskey, when I wondered if the grand gesture of a man driving cross-country through the limits of fatigue to get to me and not once getting mad at me for losing our beloved pup would be the thing to reunite us. And later, when he was there and the dog was there and I remembered why we weren't together anymore, I wondered if that was the lesson, that Jack got lost to give me courage, to remind me of the strength that comes from knowing exactly what to do to care for yourself, no matter how harsh the conditions. Running for home, against every conceivable odd: could there *be* anything more symbolic?

But maybe Jack just got out, *and then* something else happened, *and then* something else (an email saying I was about to contact a lawyer)—a series of events, this-then-that, rather than this-*so-that*. Milton staunchly denied a deterministic universe. But that doesn't mean Jack wasn't trying to get home, fed up with eluding Campus Safety and foraging for rabbit scat and pizza crusts. It doesn't mean Jack wasn't looking for *me*. I want to be in *that* world, in fact, one that has shape but not design, where to behave intentionally is not the same as obedience and does not require the metaphysical operations of *what else*. I can choose to believe that Jack is a marvel of a dog *and* be a *heretic in the truth*, as Milton advocates in one of his political tracts, for eschewing doctrinal compliance.

There's something about amazement that in stunning us quiet seems then to impel us toward narrative arc. It's never enough to say what happened, without context or point. Mustn't we do more than shake our heads and shrug at the sheer *unbelievableness* of life? Aren't we supposed to honor it, the sorrow and joy, by giving it a frame? There's no denying Jack as a *good story*. I could commodify Jack, if I had that kind of imagination or initiative, if I knew how to parlay the *good story* into a children's book, a Broadway play, a movie, a line of merch (think t-shirts, stuffed toys, the bobble-head dashboard terrier). It made no sense that the local paper never got in touch for the feel-good headline of the holiday season. Relatives of my colleagues from coast to coast still ask after "that little dog," because the ending was happy; distances made it heroic, which is why my mother and step-dad (on whose birthday Jack was found—convergences abounding) mapped the search on Google Earth.

Three days after Jack came home, a colleague went to a Boy Scout shop to buy badges for the dog-who-could, my emblem-of-fierce. She wanted the badges for courage and for home, the one a red heart, the other a tiny hearth with a fire glowing within. The man behind the counter screwed up his eyebrows at her. "You have to *actually* be a Boy Scout to have these," he said, guarding—not unreasonably—the gates. (Later I would ponder the irony of a dog being denied these hu-man tokens of his fortitude, on the grounds of not being a legitimate member of the tribe, when you can go online and buy service-dog vests without providing a single shred of proof that your animal's been trained—which I know because Jack *is* a certified therapy dog and has the vest to prove it.)

"But these are for a dog who got lost," said my colleague, rubbing the red heart between her fingers, imagining it pinned to the argyle-sweater-that-saved-a-life.

"Oh!" said the man with the eyebrows, in the shop three towns away from where I live. Naturally I'd never met him. "You mean *Jack*?"

"Jack" was a shibboleth of sorts. "Jack" was the coin of the realm.

ROBERT LOWELL WROTE to his friend Randall Jarrell that "Dark-ness honestly lived through is a place of wonder and life." Lowell should know; he suffered notoriously. One of the websites I visited during the ordeal of Jack reassured me that what I felt as the ago-nized uncertainty of his absence, my dog was most likely enjoying as a grand adventure. It broke my heart to think of him afraid and alone in the cold, and so I *was* consoled by the idea that at that very moment, while I was reeling from yet another moment of life *turn-ing on a dime*, Jack was having the time of his life. What I was *living through*, he was simply *in*. The psychoanalysts call it going-on-being, this ability to withstand separations and loss and to accommodate the wild flux of experience. In Buddhism it's *presence*. In dog—well, you get the point: it's occupying time as a matter of the perpetually imminent good-that-can-happen. Jack was not narrating his experience to himself, imagining how he'd arrange the photos of his trip in the album or prewriting postcards in his head to spin the tale for maximum effect. I was doing that for him, still am (now I've enlisted you in the project), because I worry I'll lose it otherwise, the moral of the story, which is that it's possible to inhabit yourself meaningfully without forcing any meaning at all.

When a woman I didn't know (who was the wife of a man I didn't know, who'd caught up to my dog at a fence separating the back of a middle-school parking lot from the train tracks, where the sweater got caught)—when this woman handed me my soaking-wet dog, who'd lost 20 percent of his body weight during his crazy caper, and I wrapped him in a pink fleece blanket adorned with white paw prints, I thought he did look a little stunned—as if to say, *what the hell just happened?* We rushed him to the vet, The Man Who Is/n't My Husband and I, where it was determined that Jack had no cuts, no breaks, no dehydration or hypothermia, no injuries of any kind. He was of course massively fatigued, slept for most of the next twenty-four hours, and when he was awake he did not let me out of his sight. I worry sometimes that I've hypercathected my dog, anthropomorphized him out of all canine recognition, transmitted to him my anxious-attachment problems, my *primal panic,* and spoiled him (I trust you caught the detail of the pink fleece). But then I look at him, paws lined up like an Egyptian tapestry, and remember what he's capable of.

When I look up the phrase "the fullness of time" (which comes to mind on the pristine buttery evenings of early summer, Jack reading the local news along grasses and shrubs—my husband dubbed it, though Milton would roll in his grave, pee-mail—and I contemplate what happens when you spend a day so quietly you begin to wonder if you're alone in the universe), I am surprised to discover that it comes from Galatians: "When the fullness of the time was come, God sent forth his Son . . . to redeem them that were under the law" (4:4–5). Surprised because I'm sure I've never read Galatians before and because *fullness* in this context connotes a kind of pregnancy come to term, conclusion rather than anticipation, accomplishment more than possibility, which is not at all what the soft, warm air of June and a dog with his snout to the ground represent, in my mind, at all.

Have you ever watched an animal catch sight of itself in a mirror? It couldn't care less who it is. I will never know exactly why Jack bolted from my care one frigidly cold day in December, or how he managed to survive weather, predators, starvation, or traffic. The mystery of it—no matter how much we try to contain it on the loom-of-making-sense—can never be resolved in any ultimate way: there can only ever be the head-shaking wonder of it. And I wonder what it might be like to linger in that unknowing. I want to live in the fullness of four-days-in-the-woods, in the fullness of the fifth day when Jack rested and I caught a glimpse of what it means to be so fully immersed in the medium of aliveness that you forget the luxuries of home—or better, *home* takes on a whole new valence. I want to "Glide under the green wave" (4.402), "tower / The mid aerial sky" (441–42). I wish, like Eve, "A thing not undesirable, sometime" (9.824), to turn on the world my answering looks of love.

2

I CHOOSE
HAPPENSTANCE

RELIGIOUS PEOPLE, my father once told me, are happier than athe-ists. We were having dinner in the town where I live, on a school night in November. He had come to visit me from several states away, the first visit he'd made for me since he dropped me off at college some twenty years before. He wasn't a pious man back then, so far as I knew, whatever stirrings of a certain kind of faith might have been taking hold in him. I still beheld him as the unbelieving psychologist I grew up with, child of Russian Jews who themselves spurned religion in the wake of the Second World War. The Christian who sat across from me that night was someone I didn't entirely recognize, even if he was, in a familiarly impulsive fashion, half-shouting at me to marry a man who couldn't possibly have been less equipped to make me happy.

I did eventually get married, years later, to a different man, so much better suited to me, and being an atheist has nothing to do with why I'm heading toward divorce—a turn-about I absolutely did not see coming. I took seriously the vows I wrote for our wedding. Not be-lieving in marriage as a sacrament, being suspicious of the normative power the institution exerts, being a child of divorce fully versed in dismal statistics—none of that means I didn't enter marriage commit-ted to the promise of forever. Even the profound unhappiness of our beginnings (oh, the weight of it: how could I possibly be good enough as someone's *wife*?, I buckled every day under the stink of my own inadequacy) or the year I was sure we were doomed, so badly were we communicating—none of that compromised the pledge I understood myself to have made to another human being. I didn't need religion to feel that I owed the man I loved the good faith of my best effort. But had I practiced some *religious* faith, would I have been happier all along? And if I had that faith the day our marriage collapsed, would the cataclysm have softened?

It would have been helpful, surely, in the confused and lachrymose state into which I plunged when we separated, to call on *belief.* Not just conviction of a moral high ground, but spiritual consolation— which is synchronicity, which is your heart beating in concert with something greater. Like Elizabeth Bishop in her poem "One Art," I'd lost "cities," a "continent"—Canada (where he is from), and Italy (where we'd planned to retire). I'd lost a family in his family. I'd lost rituals of cooking, caring for Jack the dog, the companionable rhythm of errands. I'd lost the hope I had for a certain kind of burnished love, one you work on steadily for years until it fits in your palm like a stone your thumb has been rubbing for luck (we had a love of stones in common, too, from pocket-sized to slate paths to rock gardens, piles of them everywhere). For years I had longed to find spiritual comfort without the requirement of spiritual belief, and now that impulse was acute. In the face of actions and implications that hurt me, in that bafflement, I longed to be rearrayed along a recognizable narrative arc. This is what we do when circumstances elude our ability to comprehend or control: we seek answers and explanations in stories that assure us that something better can and *will* happen next. Since one of the worst effects of separation was the loss of a particular future, I felt desperate to know the new ending, the last page of the text we were no longer crafting in tandem, that seemed now to be written in invisible ink.

I can't say my husband and I split up because he strove to be happy and I was stuck going in and out of what my therapist calls "the rumination door," every so often down into a rabbit-hole-of-my-own-making, but it factored. I come from an illustrious line of brooders from whom I'm sure I gleaned that love means never having to say *I'm happy.* For a long time I thought that even admitting to a sensation of happiness was somehow suspect, requiring suppression of life's painful truths and associated with the false highs of adolescence, love, hormones, or drugs. (Can you imagine living with such a person? My husband hardly could. "Spending time with a depressed person is enervating," says Meri Nana-Ama Danquah with delicious understatement in her memoir *Willow Weep for Me* [217]). The introspective self, after all—have I gotten this so wrong?—cannot elude its own shadows. Years ago my sister sent me two *New Yorker* cartoons I now have framed on my desk. In one, a diner in a restaurant says to the waiter, "Excuse me—I think there's something wrong with this in a tiny way that no one other than me would ever be able to pinpoint." In the other, a doctor asks his patient, "Would you describe the pain everyone else causes you as dull and throbbing or sharp like a knife?" I used to wave these before my husband as a plea of sorts: to understand that I was not so strange, and to stop trying to make me, even as I wished, really wished, he *could* make me, happy. Because he often told me—like a mantra but sometimes it felt like a weapon—that he organized his life around the imperative of happiness. It came up time and again, and especially in the first months after we separated: his idea that happiness was a person's "just due," nearly a Jeffersonian birthright, that provided him with a sense of purpose. Even the Dalai Lama would agree: "We are made to seek happiness," he is quoted as saying in a book on the so-called Art of that emotion (52). "Every one of us has the basis to be happy."

But I thought the notion of an endpoint, striving toward a goal, was antithetical to the Buddhist principle of inhabiting the present moment, receptive to the fluctuations of *what is* without constantly referring experience to the sense-making machine of our critical minds. And shouldn't happiness be free from debt to any organizing system? If we find happiness only according to the precepts and instructions of belief, can we trust it as real, or is it simply learned, the benefit of an ideology that purports to answer all our questions, quelling the puzzles of existence? But maybe that's philosophically naïve; Socrates, for whom the "unexamined life" was famously "not worth living," associated happiness precisely with adherence to ideals of virtue, and so with strength of character far more than varieties of circumstance. And even Freud, that grump—who rejected entirely religion's claim to be the single source of our happiness—allowed as we might find a little satisfaction in the fulfillment of instinct. Even my father, knowing me as his unhappy godless daughter and worried for my well-being (if also the state of my soul), once told me there was no point living a life so low and gently steered me toward the antidepressants that would eventually lighten my mood.

In all of this lies some conundrum about happiness as an innate capacity or a derivative of structures of meaning. There's brain chemistry, and conviction, and the question of choice. Oh, I've wanted to believe in agency; I thought that's what all the therapy was for, the endless talking-through designed to unearth original pain. I've been waiting a long time for that kind of revelatory change, the elusive promise of a self-help world. My husband believed it too—that he could fix what ailed me, that I could become (at least) happy-adjacent. I've also struggled to understand, and to agree with, the Buddhist notion that *self* is so much dandelion fluff borne on the air, and that in turn we can disentangle ourselves from the worry, inhibition, anxiety, and fear that tend to dominate our thinking. That *does* sound joyous, shucking the old depressive tales retold through years of habit. What a relief it would be, not to loathe oneself so forcefully! Between the psychoanalysis of my younger days, then (repair the primal wound), and the secular mindfulness I quasi-practice (nothing needs fixing), how to soothe that sense of dis-ease that Milton's Eve calls, in a moment of frantic despair at the perceived dissolution of her marriage, "languish[ing] without hope" (10.995)?

Well, that's the muddle.

At the end of one of my favorite essays by Nancy Mairs, the author announces that she chooses joy. It's a loaded moment. Mairs battled depression for years, attempted suicide more than once, and had multiple sclerosis, a condition whose frustrations she acknowledged frankly, though she was also a steadfast advocate of disability rights and among the first to reclaim *crippled* as a designation of community and pride. Her themes are raw, bold, and utterly human: death, sex, sadness, the embarrassments of being embodied—and also, increasingly as she aged, the redemptions of faith and the possibilities of transcendent, if always emphatically mortal, joy. She insisted on joy as a choice. That kind of joy is separate from satisfaction, and Mairs offers it not as the effect of something we might buy or consume, but as something we already have within us, a quality of being we can nurture in ourselves.

I'm not quite there yet, with Mairs, secure in a promise that life, ordinary struggle-filled life, will "recompense" us with joy, as Milton's Adam also reassures Eve (10.1052). For now, from the place I am, in the felt incoherence of a separation that endures, I'm choosing a different worldview. Call it happenstance.

PARADISE LOST IS FULL of reference to happenstance. The very cosmos thrums with it. Human history is set in motion less by the static category of "evil" than by the "ill chance" of a "strong rebuff" of wind that catches Satan as he plummets through a "vast vacuity," his wings rendered useless, beyond the gates of hell (1.932–36); without that gust he'd still be falling. He is likened in size to leviathan "haply slumbering" on the ocean—"haply" suggesting both *circumstance* and *contentment*—happened upon by a sailor who takes the whale for an island and anchors against him for a night (1.203). (Appearances are everywhere deceiving in Milton's oeuvre.) The fallen angels wonder if God reigns supreme only by chance (1.133). What is longed for in this world is frequently chanced upon, never guaranteed; desires are equally often foiled by chance. The losses of holy war are avenged by the "odds" of divine wisdom. Eve understands Adam to be preeminent by so much "odds" (4.447). The word denotes her awareness of his authority in the scheme of things but implies a haphazard lack of proportion. Forms of "happy" throughout the poem—from *hap*, meaning *chance*, and also *lucky*, which means *occurring by chance*, in a fortuitous circularity—tell us not to take happiness for granted. Its very ubiquity reminds us of how closely it sits to the absence of agency and control. It comes, when and if it comes at all, borne by the wind.

Even the very nature of being seems vaguely arbitrary in this apparently orderly universe. Moments after eating the apple in book 9, Eve wonders if she should keep what she's done secret from Adam, to safeguard a newfound power located in the "odds" of knowledge. By *odds* she means the sudden discrepancy between what she knew before and what she knows now, between herself and Adam. She also implies that if knowledge is power, it's only by chance that Adam ever had more of it than she did. Eve is a woman in a man's world, a student of nature whose husband discounts her expertise even as he complains that the garden mocks his own efforts to tend it, the younger sister of an anxious brother not quite convinced of the priority everyone keeps telling him he enjoys. To share the apple with Adam would be to "partake / Full happiness" with him, but momentarily more enticing is the thought of having no "copartner" at all in the pleasure of pursuing her thoughts, unimpeded by Adam's fretting and nervous adherence to doctrine. Cautiously, stiltedly, Eve sidles up to the possibility that to be "more equal," to be "sometime / Superior," *might*, "perhaps," be "A thing not undesirable . . . for inferior who is free?" (9.823–25). But then a worse thought occurs, that she might die for her rash devouring, and Adam, in her extinction, "wedded to another" (828). That's the scare she cannot risk—losing a love it seems clear in another dozen lines or so she did not fully believe she could trust.

The point of all this, this story of how we began in a Chaos that swirls around us (immortal beings buffeted by the wind!) is Milton's fierce conviction in an indeterminate universe. God foresees but does not preordain, a situation rather like knowing a toddler is about to fall backward in her chair but having done nothing to cause the imminent crash. But there's a reason the God of his epic has struck so many readers as both monarchical and adolescent, greedy in his need for uncoerced expressions of love and adamant, like any teen, in his righteousness. This poetic God, some have said, is Milton's denigration of earthly kings who wrested power to themselves and evacuated their subjects of the capacity for rational choice. We are nothing without our power to decide for ourselves. It's neither erotic helplessness nor uxorious weakness that "fixe[s]" Adam's lot to Eve's (9.952), propelling him to eat the apple, but a loyal if melancholy commitment to the woman from whose "sweet converse" he will not be "severed." The fact that their marriage has been beset by disagreements about work, independence, duty, and notions of food storage (Milton's first couple, brilliantly, have entirely ordinary squabbles) only heightens the significance of his choosing. It also obliterates any easy faith in Edenic bliss. To put it bluntly, paradise is a fiction. Long before Satan mists himself into the body of an otherwise innocent snake in the garden, the thoroughly human Adam and Eve have been struggling to negotiate the differences between them—to say nothing of an autocratic

God and his posse of spies. Eating the apple constitutes a bid for *divergence* from a single garden path. As William Empson once wrote, it's their only viable mode of escape.

The radical turning point of a life, *Paradise Lost* teaches us, is not contrition or confession but biting into self-authorship beside the one you love. Adam and Eve are a stronger couple for the daring act they undertake together. After the apple comes not immediate demise (what they thought "Was meant by death that day" [10.1050]), nor even spiritual rebirth, but "pangs" and a "second groan" (9.1001): nature giving birth to herself so they can start all over again on different terms. The proof of this comes in Adam's freewheeling hermeneutical spin on the punishments doled out by the Son in the wake of transgression. Toiling in sorrow, eating in sorrow, bearing children in sorrow, cursed with a final end as dust in the ground: it is Adam's best and most audacious moment to rewrite these sentences so thoroughly that they are no longer recognizable as penalty, comforting Eve with a vision of what he calls "commodious" life. Nearly recklessly—except that the poem endorses this fantasy of the future—Adam turns the Son's pronouncement of hardship into meaningful work, fleeting physical pain, inventive solutions to the threat of cold, the two of them culminating not *as* dust but *in* dust, which a rejuvenated Adam can finally imagine not as an adversarial garden but rather his "native home" (10.1085).

This is not happiness, I think, but *fullness*. The sense of belonging that Buddhism, too, locates in feeling at home.

REMEMBER WHEN WE found out about "Scandinavian *hygge*" (coziness) and got addicted to *Borgen* and convinced ourselves we could fall asleep in that half-year half-light? No fewer than six books on Nordic contentment were published in 2016 alone. (Scandinavian countries, among the happiest on earth, are also the least religious, according to a recent Gallup poll.) Survey after online survey tells us where people eat the best, exercise the most, die the oldest, have the most sex, and go to church most often. One reports that the happiest US cities are clustered in the South (while all the unhappy people are in the North, which I suppose my father, who lives in Texas, would correlate with religion, horses, and family values). Another gives the prize to California—all the saintly cities—for fitness, culture, and organic produce.

It's easy to feel inundated by inducement: to volunteer, do more yoga, make more time for friends, get another guinea pig or cat. Some distinguish between the quest for transient pleasure and the cultivation of long-lasting reward. But call it what you will, we are bombarded on all sides by pressure to be upbeat and the promise of merchandising to get us there. Brooding, in this context, is downright impolite. Even the modest suggestion of journalist Dan Harris's 2014 memoir *10% Happier*, about his televised panic attack on *Good Morning America* and subsequent foray into mindfulness—get just a *little* bit more happy into our lives—is offered with breathless forward-driving narrative momentum that keeps our attention trained on the promise of "revelation" if we stick to a meditation regimen: the allure, I'd argue, of singular, epiphanical moments of awareness and release, portals to happy, if we just try hard enough.

A principle of happenstance wouldn't so much deny the possibility of intentionality—happiness as a function of *doing* something—as teach us to stay grounded in the swirls and caroms of experience when all that purposeful effort just doesn't work. I'm not opposed to being happy, either, however this sounds (or incapable of joy, another of our perennial arguments, my husband and me; he once accused me of "wallowing" when I was still sad about the death of a cat named Linc, one day after Linc died of kidney failure). It's a question of control. Hounded by vicious internal critics, gnawed at by our longings, terrified of death and our own frailty, beset by circumstance, we try to stabilize, we activate *willpower*, we "think happy thoughts." But happiness can't be fabricated. A sailor my parents knew when I was in high school once told me that the key to avoiding seasickness is not to resist the rise and fall of the boat. The more you relax your body into the waves, the less you clench against that sensation—unpredictable and yet entirely guaranteed—the less you want to wretch, or cry, or die.

Of course, some situations can't be ridden out like a bad but survivable storm. The point isn't that we're helpless to act, or not allowed to *want*, as we get tossed from side to side in our chaotic, indeterminate lives. It's that when we get tangled up in expectations about how things ought to be (think of Adam and Eve at the knees of heavenly beings, given to understand their proper roles and reprimanded when they stray from the hierarchy of it all), when we orient exclusively on some future "happy end" (that's the archangel Michael's term, late in *Paradise Lost*), when we resist pain at all costs and deny the fullest range of what we can feel—yes, even and also the happiness—well, maybe and paradoxically, that's when we lose our way. I had my idea of what marriage was *supposed* to be like, and he had his. We couldn't agree; we couldn't find the words. And then, when the bottom fell out and I floundered in grief, it was hard not to feel rent by pointlessness. Why had either of us tried so hard to get it right, when we couldn't articulate our longings or follow the scripts we'd dog-eared in desperation? I'd wanted a mature love, I thought I'd chosen *character* over *charisma*. In the event we both tried too hard to make the other change.

I recognize the irony that I'm indulging here, crafting an organized system out of happenstance.

IN HIS LAST NOVEL, left uncompleted before he killed himself in 1961, called *The Garden of Eden*, Ernest Hemingway writes that *happiness in intelligent people is the rarest thing I know*. An ex of mine sent me that line ages ago, and I taped it to the wall above where I work. Tradition has it that Hemingway's widow stuffed the pages of the manuscript in a tote bag and carried them to Scribner's, which would publish a heavily and controversially abridged edition of the book fifteen years later. Its protagonists are a writer, David Bourne, and his wife, Catherine, on honeymoon in France and Spain, who entangle themselves in a tortured *ménage* with the beautiful Marita. It's the 1920s, Catherine cuts her hair short like a boy's, she and David are blond and tan, like *brothers*, she thinks; he calls her "Devil"; at night she fingers him and describes their gender-play, her acts of taking him, him being the girl, as *the change*. The wording is stilted—*no one would say that*, I think to myself, when she tells him after making love, "You were so good to change"—but it gets at something complicated in simple terms (Hemingway's own edict as a writer, to *know how complicated it is and then state it simply*). The hair's-breadth between happiness and dissatisfaction. How quickly into the dream we yearn all over again for newness. Married three weeks, the youthful bride wildly in love, bristling too (like Eve) at the priority of her husband's artistic success, the boredom of being a housewife, the constraints of a body that from the beginning she tries in every way to transform, she sets about trying to turn them both into something different.

They drink absinthe. They drink whiskey, wine, and vermouth. They swim in the ocean, fish for bass, drive to Biarritz, tan themselves as dark as possible, sleep naked. If not a garden, then paradisal *presence,* mere waftings of the future nagging at David's consciousness, what might happen when he gets back to work, if the second book will be as well-received as the first. He thinks, *It was a very simple world and he had never been truly happy in any other. . . . There was only happiness and loving each other and then hunger and replenishing and starting over* (14). By *starting over* he means *repeat;* he thinks he wants *just this* with Catherine over and over, but by the end of the novel it means expulsion, out of an Eden that was never truly any happier than Milton's; it means David not with Catherine but the lover Marita, because the Eve-girl, independent apple-eater full of guilt for the havoc she's wreaked, has blown off to Paris to try to make amends. She has burned every scrap of David's writing that doesn't concern her.

Between my father and Hemingway is a kind of Epimenedes Paradox, where if religious people are happy and intelligent people are not, religious people must not be intelligent. But this is obviously wrong; and anyway, the point of the quote—the reason my ex sent it to me, and I taped it to my wall—wasn't about smarts, it was about feeling we needed to accept unhappiness as a condition of temperament. It's true my father seems happier—at least, much less discontent—since he became actively religious. Was Hemingway chronically unhappy? It's well known that he attacked life voraciously. John Walsh, in the UK *Independent* in 2011, called Hemingway a *"rumbustious* man of action." Hemingway converted to Catholicism when he married for the second time. Some say he was religious but not observant. Others say the piety of his work has been diminished by literary critics. The Celebrity Atheist List claims him as one of their own. "Our nada who art in nada, nada be thy name," says the eighty-year-old narrator of "A Clean Well-Lighted Place"; in his memoir *A Moveable Feast,* Hemingway wrote that "all thinking men are atheists." One biographer says that Hemingway believed religion to be a "menace" to happiness. In a letter to his mother, Hemingway claimed to pray every night.

It's mordantly ironic to name a book about jealousy, vindictiveness, and failure "The Garden of Eden." Of *course* there's no paradise in this novel, despite the beautiful landscapes, the lovely bodies, the expensive automobiles, the fresh fish, and buckets of unholy water they down at the bar. Despite David's insistence on the repetition of happiness or the ecstatic pleasures of role-play and corporeal excess. But maybe the macho Hemingway wanted to imagine being other than himself, to start again, just like his David—not in the repetitiousness of immature love but by writing an alternative origin of things, through queer physicality and sexual and racial experimentation. Biblical references these days will always function metafictionally (think of Toni Morrison's *Song of Solomon,* or Marilynne Robinson's *Gilead*): the minute you hear one you know what's at stake, whatever your religious proclivity. The whole history of the phrase will unfurl behind it; we read one text through our memories of others, through layers of social, theological, literary meaning. Hemingway's title points us toward everything we think we know about this tale and then veers off into the thickets of its own preoccupations, the religion of writing, the higher aspiration of art. And that of course is the point: everything's in the retelling. *Know how complicated it is and then tell it simply.*

In any true garden of Eden, both Hemingway and Milton suggest, happiness equals change equals choice. That doesn't mean we choose to be happy over sad, as if it were so easy. It means that we fully inhabit our lives only when we have the freedom to think for ourselves and make our own decisions. There's a difference between asking someone to alter, or amending ourselves out of disgust with who we are—change as a form of disguise (*You were so good to . . .*)—and embracing the kind of motion that comes from curiosity, wonderment, discovery. A difference between a frantic search *for* happiness and the kind of imaginative learning that happens even when experience hurts. For Milton, this means liberation from tyrannical, monarchical rule. Happiness, if there is such a thing, cannot coexist with the stasis he associated with being told what to do. *Perpetuall progression* is the rallying cry, in one of his political tracts. From the very beginning of *Paradise Lost*, "our grand parents" are in motion (1.29).

YOU'LL HAVE NOTICED that I do not refer to eating the apple as The Fall. This is not mere irreligious stubbornness. Milton himself makes of that word an overdetermined lexical node, for falling in *Paradise Lost* is almost always a physical act, and yet every instance of it will necessarily call a reader's attention to the meaning of spiritual collapse. Or more exactly, to the frames and conditions whereby something is styled a sin. To fall is not always to fail. Adam and Eve fall to prayer, to eating a meal, to their knees. Mulciber (or Vulcan, or Hephaestus, choose your worldview), architect of Pandemonium, is fabled to have fallen for a day, dropping "from the zenith like a falling star," when Jove throws him out of heaven (1.745). Even the fallen angels are literal: at the end of the war in heaven, chucked out of that ethereal quintessence, they fall "headlong" through the sky to the fiery lakes of hell (1.45). When is one fall not like another?

The lure of a fall as the index of sinfulness is that it is so bodily a metaphor. Children fall, and the aged and infirm; we fall down drunk; we fall to pieces; to fall is to lose one's bearings, to be lowered in anyone's estimation: it is action that occurs in space, it demarcates—to fall is to no longer stand—and it differentiates, hierarchically: I am looking up, while you are looking down. That sense of strict division, happiness from regret, transgression from redemption, is precisely what Milton's epic complicates, since characters are more often in the process of falling than fallen. Whatever it means to hit bottom, we aren't there yet; human experience is one of suspension in the condition of getting somewhere. We *will* be buffeted by the wind.

But how do we react? Every waking moment of every day, I tell my students, places you at the brink of decision, all alone, with only your own resources at hand. Ask yourself, I say, *What would Milton do?* This is often the moment when they fall in love with him, because as scary as it seems, the idea that we are responsible to an inward ethical compass—but thoroughly so, and informed by the kind of voluminous reading that Milton had done—is ultimately empowering. "Let us not think / Hard," says Adam in one of the poem's most awesome and ironic of enjambments (4.432–33), a line break that completely undercuts his blustery instruction to Eve to take lightly the injunction against eating of the Tree of Knowledge of Good and Evil by seeming to plead with her for the freedom to just quit thinking altogether. But this we cannot abdicate, the tough contemplation of whom we want to be *right now*, in lonely but glorious choosing. Milton, who famously argued in a sonnet that "they also serve who only stand and wait," needed to believe that deep rumination and the art that came from it would count as worthy of God's respect, and he urged his readers to rely on themselves, not the consolations of doctrine, as the only way to work through the most complicated and urgent questions of existence.

It's a chaotic world, and we're alone at the precipice. But to put it that way isn't to imply we can ignore the responsibility of our relationships. Choices only matter because they ripple outward from ourselves. Milton understood that; it's why his Eve and his Adam cogitate on everything they do through the complex terms of their mutual engagement, even as they strive toward the fullest expression of independence. "Make good choices," I say to students at the end of class, especially on Thursdays when the enticements of a weekend beckoned and I worry, not for their souls but for what they'll feel the morning after, waking up to the brute fact of themselves. I don't necessarily mean that they should refrain from the sex they want to have or the booze they'll surely drink (though Milton would have); it isn't the *adjective* I'm thinking of so much as the *verb*. Do the hard work, I might say, before you decide, and consider the effects on others. To *debauch* is to disperse, the very etymology of the word connoting separation and rupture. In this sense bad behavior defiles only because it tears us away from more reinforcing loves.

One afternoon, backing down the driveway on my way to a couples therapy session, I flashed on what it must have felt like to him, my husband, putting his own car in reverse toward an assignation with *her*, the woman I cannot name, off to a tryst somewhere, maybe in the cellar of the restaurant he'd opened against my strong objections, and where she once helped out by tending bar. (I will forever remember the glimpse I got, of a woman with short dark hair and funky black glasses, as I walked past toward the kitchen.) My whole body ignited with arousal and rage. I was looking at the fence he'd put up, at my request, along the edge of the yard, at the California slate he'd used to cover over the hideous weathered brick at the front of the house, and I could feel it precisely in every pore, the exquisite, sickening rush of anticipation of a thing you want to do, that you *will* do, knowing it's wrong no matter how clever the rationale you've concocted for yourself. The heart-pounding eagerness for it, the delight and relief of having set it in motion, of being in motion toward it. So palpable was my grasp in that moment of how much he had wanted her—so total the pain of it—that I nearly lost control of the car.

Somehow, despite my perseverant thinking about how to make a relationship "work," we'd fallen apart, my husband and I, one especially difficult year, fallen into ruts and a tacit agreement to avoid the tougher truths of our mistrust of each other, and so they fell in love. And when, after a time, things fell back into place (years before I knew about the affair), we didn't triumphantly rise into remedy or correction, he and I, made no conscious choice; we simply got on with the routine matters of a marriage. Had someone tumbled headlong down, forsaking the better parts of himself? Was it that, in our humanness, we all forgot the imperative to pause a moment in the tugging, pressing wind and think/hard about how *this moment* might alter the course of a life? Had we substituted the dramatic gratifications of pleasure, argument, and momentum for the subtler adjustments to environment and to each other that defines Eve's spirit of curiosity and wonder? That is *true* contentment? In one version of the myth of happiness, we have to be brought low to guarantee ascent toward a fulfillment we regard as—well, I'll say it again: nearly a kind of birthright. Could it be that we were destined to a dramatic crash as the precursor of a richer, more fulfilling involvement?

But *Paradise Lost* defies these spatial, and causal, logics. All beings are subject to the happenstance of experience. For a time, I wished fervently to believe that my husband, "undone" as he told me he was by the loss of us, would sort himself out, turn a proverbial new leaf, and that we would rebound into a love made stronger by surviving its own destruction. Instead the months dragged on. Neither of us could let the other off the hook, nor fully let go.

It's the central paradox of the poem that Milton's human pair seem most at ease, most contented, in the ambiguity of an epic ending that—even though we know their future—gives us Adam and Eve in a radically open-ended present moment, in the process of making their way.

I'VE KNOWN MILTON for so long that Adam and Eve might be just as important to my ideas about marriage as my own parents. Milton well understood that no matter how desperately we want to believe we're meant for each other (*soul of my soul*, Adam calls Eve), we will jealously guard what's ours (*from my side subducting, took perhaps / More than enough*); the funniest moments in *Paradise Lost* may be when the pair try to impress upon each other just how bad it feels when their needs aren't met. I've often thought it a miracle that any couple stays together for any length of time. How can two people *not* visit upon each other everything they need by way of reparation—for woundedness, say, at the hands of hapless, hippie parents who had two kids before they were twenty-five? Except that miracle suggests intercession, and for Milton, anyway, nothing intervenes except hard-won human effort.

Milton knew what he was up to when he placed the Holy Spirit, "Dove-like," to "broo[d] on the vast abyss" and hatch the world (1.21). Part of what makes any explanatory myth so attractive is its promise that someone will one day *know*, that we will no longer have to explain ourselves, that all the repellent bits of ourselves might be witnessed and forgiven. Isn't this what drives any couple to marital therapy, the wife to self-compassion retreats and the husband to, perhaps, *elsewhere:* not feeling recognized? (Experts say that couples typically land in therapy six years too late, which means my husband and I should have started therapy on our honeymoon.) Paradise, such as Adam and Eve inhabited it, was an abstraction—like death—that they had learned but never lived. That disjunction, between being told they were in it without experiential proof of actually enjoying it, is, I think, what makes many a marriage founder in the shoals. I married my husband because I wanted to learn to choose joy, but I didn't grasp until too late how his philosophy of happiness was crafted to shield a traumatized little boy still suffering within the man, and still I held to a notion of sadness as somehow more real. The well of it inside me was simply antithetical to the well of good feeling he thought a married couple had a duty to honor and preserve.

That's a binary no two people can happily occupy, and it flattens the truth of what we did achieve together, the myriad pleasures and solace of dailiness, the learning we tried to do for each other, about each other. Happiness is what it sounds like, as Milton comprehended: largely happenstance, even if choice means we have the freedom to turn toward the world, into what lies before us. And to rescind that insidious false creed, that love means getting to behave at your worst, almost without consequences. This is what I want to believe, in the end, about Miltonic love: two people, separate subjects each, doing that hard work. Confident in their affection, needing nothing from one another but a wide companionable space in which to wander, make mistakes, and forgive.

3

INTO THE WORLD
BEFORE US

THE SEPARATION HAPPENED, suddenly, on a Wednesday at the start of August, six years into marriage. There've been only a few times in my life where I can honestly say that *everything changed* in an instant, but this was one of them: we were married, and then I confronted him with a string of texts I'd read on his phone (yes, that happened too), and then we weren't—not in the same way.

Maybe it's time to explain. That one terrible spring, when we'd been married three years, I went to therapy, and my husband went to refurbish a kitchen for a woman he'd once dated, and at the end of a long day of work, over a celebratory glass of wine, she climbed into his lap and kissed him. And he, because he'd felt demoralized and disregarded and misunderstood by me, also felt vindicated in that moment, then *came home* to me, as he would think of it, that night and many other times for more than two years, until the day we were in the ER, he and I, having long since emerged—so I thought—from that dark and uncommunicative place, because his gall bladder was inflamed and he'd had triple bypass surgery literally a week before. I was nursing my man, I thought; we were moving into an era of better health and happiness. I had his phone, picked it up to reply to the manager of my husband's restaurant as my husband writhed in the ER bed, loaded on morphine and Dilaudid, and my eye caught a row of *x*'s and *o*'s to or from (what's the difference?) a woman whose name I recognized because they were friends; I didn't know they'd once dated. I didn't know they *were* dating, if that's not entirely the wrong word for two people who find love and sustain love as a series of elaborate obfuscations and lies.

One afternoon not long after my husband was gone, I wandered from room to room in the house, literally searching for something. That kind of restlessness is a symptom of depression, if you want to frame it that way, or you could call it a spiritual wandering, compelled by unbearable doubt. I went to my bedroom, whose walls I had painted pale yellow to remake the space in my image, then to the guest room, where his underwear and socks (still there, months later) seemed to spring at me from the bureau like Jack-in-the-boxes, and shirts and pants dangled eerily in the closet. He'd used that room as a dressing chamber of sorts, slept in there when his snoring got bad, and it reeked of cologne that had leached into the panels of a dresser drawer. I remembered his sister-in-law—also, once, my sister-in-law—telling me that when she had separated briefly from her husband (his brother, my brother-in-law, all of us hyphenated in love), she would wrap herself in his winter jackets and lie down on their bed to cry. So I tried that, too, pulling around me a dress shirt three sizes too big to get him on me again, a smell, cells of skin, anything, reviving or entombing myself in these imprecise analogies of presence.

I knew that answers would not come to me from any god. I had never believed, not like that. But two days a week I clambered into the lifeboat of Milton, and for the life of me, I taught.

MILTON HAD NEVER MADE as much sense to me as he did that fall. No: I had never *felt* Milton so much as I did that fall. I had to take fall semester off from chairing my department, such a wreck was I, and I didn't have the energy, some days, to lift myself off the couch to get to school much earlier than ten minutes before the start of class. I was squatting in the office of a colleague on sabbatical. The sight of my books and tchotchkes overflowing from cardboard boxes on the floor seemed an ominous metaphor for the state of myself. I was rocked entirely by what seemed impossible to explain. *How did it happen?* I didn't recognize the view from this office I was interloping in; the angle of absolutely everything was wrong. But something got righted again when I crossed the threshold into class.

From my state of disoriented hurt, how could Milton fail to move me, poet of heretical independence for whom the confusion of the universe was *promising*, full of discovery and charge? We rode the wave of his revolutionary zeal, my students and I, the urgency of Milton's life-on-the-line conviction, the magic of his ideas suspended, crystalline and pendant, in hundreds of lines of verse, all semester long. It wasn't just intellectual arousal. It was the wild alchemy of students falling in love with a poet I love before my eyes. The surprise of witnessing, once again, how much this writer, whose potential irrelevance to my students I had acknowledged on day one, could still matter so much to them as they made their way, halting and bold alike, through their lives. The crucible of a classroom in which I was reading my life in Milton, living my story through Milton in the company of students thoroughly galvanized by the currency and aliveness of his thinking. The minute I walked through the door to those expectant faces that had wrestled with the writer all night, the panic of my current circumstance would subside. I was recognizable to myself as a reader of *Comus*, "Lycidas," *Paradise Lost*, even if I'd lost the shape of myself as "wife." I've always believed that literary criticism is a form of autobiography. I wasn't just teaching Milton. I was being me-in-Milton.

Milton himself became a private teacher as a young man in the 1640s, after his return from a lengthy sojourn in Italy. His first pupils were nephews Edward and John Phillips, the sons of his sister Anne, who came to live with him at rented lodgings in London when they were only nine and ten; he subsequently established a small school. Milton's early thinking about education, laid out in a brief treatise on the subject in 1644, engaged with other intellectuals pushing for radical pedagogical reform, but it seems arid and doctrinaire in a way that's hard to square with the resistant, oppositional habits of mind so evident in his other writing of the time. It's in Milton's correspondence with boyhood friend Charles Diodati that learning is more passionately defined, not as an institutionalized program of study but as a corollary of erotic (if platonic) friendship. In their writings to and about each other, Milton and Diodati describe an almost physical need, like hunger, to search for the beautiful in tandem with another like-minded soul—as if, in isolation from that partnership, knowledge has no meaning, nearly doesn't exist. This is why *Paradise Lost* consistently figures knowledge as a process of learning from those who delight you: why it's Raphael, "the sociable spirit" (5.221), dispatched to earth to discourse with Adam and Eve, why Adam then can't get enough of the "sweetness" of conversation with the angel (8.216) and why Eve (though only after several thousand lines) returns to her garden, preferring to mix her "high dispute" with Adam's "conjugal caresses" (8.55–56). Learning is a charged affair.

Milton also, of course, knew a thing or two about divorce. His first marriage, at thirty-four, to seventeen-year-old Mary Powell is by now notorious for the juicy detail that Mary returned to live with her mother after just a month with John—evidence of some incompatibility it's hard not to feel the pressure of in his heretical *Doctrine and Discipline of Divorce,* one of three tracts written in defense of calling it quits. There's no definitive explanation for Mary's departure. Edward Phillips, who became one Milton's earliest biographers, tells us that John "took Journey into the Country" and came home a month later "a Married-man, that went out a Batchelor," and the divorce tract does, enticingly, ask its readers to reconsider the wisdom of forcing two people who hardly knew each other when they married to stay yoked in an unworkable union. Phillips further speculates that Mary felt lonely in John's bookish household; her family were Royalists, moreover, at a time when Milton had begun his polemical career and the country was on the brink of civil war. Biographers caution against making too strict a correlation between his travails with Mary Powell and Milton's arguments about divorce, against a too-simple idea that the intellectual Milton would only be motivated to tackle the religious and philosophical implications of divorce because of a highly intimate set of personal problems. But surely their differences of opinion mattered.

In Milton's ingenious argument, divorce *honors* marriage by protecting the fundamental principles of what a good relationship is: a relief and a cure for loneliness in the pleasure of two minds joining. "Forbidden to divorce," he writes in this impassioned plea for sympathy from the legislators of matrimonial law (874), we are in effect also "forbidden to marry," because a marriage that violates God's purpose for it is no marriage at all. What's the point of a regulation that, in making adultery the sole justification for divorce, thereby makes a mockery of marriage as a shell-corporation for sex? How can we endorse a law that practically sanctions infidelity by compelling loyalty to an unhappy union? Sometimes we act rashly, Milton insists—as when we're young, and how can we know what we're in for when there's no such thing as living together in 1644? (Without "freedom of access," as he puts it, we're deprived of "a perfect discerning till too late" [873].) Why should we be stuck forever with a bad choice, especially if staying married to avoid the supposed sin of divorce would drive us to worse transgressions? No reasonable person could ratify such a law, one that promotes misbehavior by failing to protect the divine gift of marriage as a source of solace.

Thus the defense of divorce is the promotion of an ideal. Milton is blunt and categorical on this score: "In Gods intention a meet and happy conversation is the chiefest and the noblest end of marriage" (871). No marriage can possibly satisfy our physical desires or quell a "God-forbidden loneliness" (872) in the absence of psychological attunement. Think of the couples you know (I imagine you are) who seem so "unsuitable" (875) to each other, their "faculties of understanding and conversing" (873) so incompatible—the ones you see at restaurants eating dinner in silence. Downtrodden couples laboring in "melancholy despair . . . though they understand it not, or pretend other causes because they know no remedy." How they contort themselves, in other words, from within their deep unhappiness, to deny the simple truth of not especially liking each other! When all that heartache could be explained by the fact of a "spiritless mate," and cured by easy access to divorce.

Conversation as it's used in his divorce tracts does not have precisely the dual meaning of *intercourse*, but Milton does make such connotations clear, as in *Paradise Lost* when he refers to the mind-body simultaneity of a "rational delight" (8.391). Adam and Eve, at their best, enjoy a fully corporeal dialogue: they talk while eating, garden while talking, look at, touch, and taste each other even in the midst of elevated discussion; the narrator (sly scamp) explains that Eve prefers talking to Adam over archangels not because she isn't intellectual enough for heavenly discourse but because "from his lip / Not words alone pleased her" (8.56–57). Even the angel Raphael, actually blushing "rosy red" (8.619), admits that his sort get a kick out of their queer commingling, especially since they can do so with their whole celestial selves, unencumbered by any clumsy "obstacle" of "membrane, joint, or limb": their brand of "union" is pure and "Total" (8.624–25, 627).

That's what I thought true love would be—secure, reliable, intersubjective *knowing*. But oh, what we inflict on each other with our unreasonable expectations! Puzzling through such questions out loud in a room with two dozen twenty-year-olds, most of them seniors poised on the brink of the rest of their lives, knowing their existential angst, feeling the heat of their anxiety about adulthood, at the same time that my own life was eluding my control, was at once awful and immensely reassuring. It embarrassed me, realizing how much I hadn't known about how to be married, all that I had gotten wrong about the man I'd married, and the vast sense of error about myself, my arrogant certitude. It had been humiliating, the email that went out from the dean of faculty in hot mid-August announcing to my department a change in chairship, as it had already been excruciating to tell him why I needed to step down; I hid in bed all that morning anticipating the queries, the speculation, the judgment. What authority could I then command before students on the subject of marriages, Edenic or otherwise, let alone existential truths, when I'd failed so epically to discern what was unraveling right under my nose? *The shoemaker's children wear no shoes,* my husband used to say, apropos of me being the stereotypically neurotic daughter of professional psychotherapists. But this was an unprecedented discrepancy, between life as it happened and the one I'd assumed.

Yet all of this is what made Milton *matter*, that fall, so urgently. I'd always found it a little comical, the convergence between Milton's rhetorical ingenuity in prose and his obvious personal impatience at being yoked to a woman with whom he could not have satisfying conversation. But now, the sound of a man railing against superstition and custom for producing resistance to change layered the teaching of the *Doctrine and Discipline of Divorce* with particular sadness. In Milton's dense and frustrated paragraphs I recognized myself, in the volubility that comes from feeling powerless against a stubborn, obdurate other. In Milton's very real disappointment about a marriage on the rocks I read my husband's loneliness, the anger I knew he had struggled to express and suppress, and my acute despair, the long months of an especially bad year, that we would ever figure out how to talk, really talk, again. Between Milton's advocacy of marriage as a sacred space in which two people sustain each other through companionable interrelation, and his defense of divorce as an entirely rational response to something as basic as an inability to meaningfully converse, I felt my breathtaking grief.

Milton's ideas about divorce were controversial in his own age (he was broadly attacked as a "Divorser"), but hardly so in our own. The intensity of reading him that semester came in part from knowing the risks he took for his principles. Private pain can impel us into action or bury us in indecision and remorse; Milton used his to change the world. And the gap of time heightened more than it diluted the significance of that action, lending gravity but also desperation to the issue; how is it possible, I would think, that we are still clamoring for someone to listen, that marriages still unravel because someone feels misunderstood? My husband and I had dozens of arguments, over the years, about whether or not it was reasonable to demand to be "gotten." For him, my needs in this regard amounted to a fixation, even though, feeling misunderstood himself, it somehow made sense to him to seek attunement and fulfillment elsewhere. Hadn't we acted out, in a kind of helpless dumb-show, exactly the misery that Milton was warning his audience of, centuries before? Reading Milton's complex prose demands one's utmost, intelligent attention. Witnessing my students' efforts to navigate his seemingly endless sentences—*willing* themselves to get it, then relishing those moments when meaning would suddenly emerge, obvious and profound, from the thickets of Miltonic syntax—filled me with joy. Knowing that my husband and I had failed each other at just this task of comprehension made many a class tough to get through. More than once I turned my back to them as I wrote on the chalkboard, blinking back tears.

One day I asked my students if it surprised them that a man of Milton's era could advocate so powerfully for divorce. A young woman with freckles sprayed across her cheeks and a fierce, unwieldy intelligence raised her hand. "A *man*, yes," she said, "but not Milton." I asked her to elaborate. "Milton prized autonomy," she said. "He described people who follow the rules without thinking for themselves as gluttons, swallowing without chewing. Digestion isn't just a metaphor for him—it represents our ability to break down ideas and make them a part of ourselves. So how could we stand to be in a marriage that makes us feel wretched inside?" The radical simplicity of that idea seemed to make everyone sit up a little straighter in their chairs. "No," she went on. "Life is fragile. If one or the other of you isn't happy in the marriage, you take a leap of faith for yourself."

What a prosaic interaction it is, conversing. We do it, do it sloppily, every single day. And yet so much depends upon doing better, getting it right.

FREUD DECLARES in *Civilization and Its Discontents* that "we are never so defenseless against suffering as when we love, never so hopelessly unhappy as when we have lost our loved object." The truth no one tells you about marriage ahead of time is that you'll be your absolute worst self in the company of your beloved. Marriage is a mirror held up to the monstrous core of you, the wrecking-ball of your gaping need, to mix a metaphor—except the confusion is exactly the point, exactly why it's so hard to still the workings of your suspicious imagination, convinced you're about to be forsaken/betrayed/abandoned, when love is a series of collisions between the emptiness you fear and the baggage you haul, the too-muchness of you (you've been schooled in it since childhood) against never being, or having, enough. And if, like me, you think love is supposed to repair all of that, restore you to your long-lost other half, well, you've just handed over to your *innamorato* the tools of your own unmaking.

"I love that part," another student offered in class one day, "where Satan comes up to Uriel and says, *Don't you know who I am?* And Uriel rolls his eyes and says, *Oh yeah, I know who you are.*" Archangel Uriel is the fire of god, shining with sagacity. Yet in his first encounter with Satan, even this "regent of the sun" (3.690) gets "beguiled" (689) by the dissembler, so convincing is Satan's disguise as a "stripling cherub" (636). It's only later, when Uriel espies Satan unaware of being seen and so catches the fallen angel looking "disfig-ured, more than could befall / Spirit of happy sort" (4.127–28), that the imposter is unmasked; no true emissary of heaven could sport so miserable a visage. It's actually the lesser angel Zephon, rather than Uriel, who later confronts Satan with the scathing directive to "Think not . . . thy shape the same" (4.835). "Thou resembles now," Zephon goes on, "Thy sin and place of doom obscure and foul" (4.839–40). These brief exchanges have important didactic implications: if evil can masquerade as good, and even pure angels can be deceived, it's obvious the human pair will struggle to discern the threat posed by a talking snake, even if they've been duly warned that Satan lurks in the periphery. But there's also an intriguing detail embedded here about who we are when we don't know we're being watched—about those private, uglier, hateful selves we indulge in private—and so what it means to be known, really known, by another.

Which brings me back to love, and what happens when the blush of infatuation fades and those other dimensions—not necessarily truer, just more complex—are revealed, as if helplessly, to those we most fervently wish to behold us in our most "virtuousest" guises. This is precisely Adam's concern when he complains that Eve ought to care about watching him be good. "From the influence of thy looks," he tells her, "[I] receive / Access in every virtue" (8.309–10). With her looking on, he feels himself "more wise, more watchful, stronger"; afraid of behaving shamefully in her eyes, he feels himself to "utmost vigour raise[d]" (8. 311, 314). Of course we want our beloved to wit-ness us at our best, but also to *allow* us our best by making space for the worst.

The pressure to provide can undermine even the most feminist of husbands, too, which is the very back-and-forth that more than once brings Adam and Eve to the brink of trouble. The conundrum that Milton's first man feels, acutely, is one of experiential versus doctrinal learning. When he launches into a tortured, oxymoronic speech about work, one that torques itself around impossible con-tradictions, we get a glimpse of his struggle to believe in his priority among so much evidence to the contrary. He tries to assert that it's actually a "pleasant" task to tend a garden that "mock[s]" him with its "unsightly," "wanton" growth (4.625–31), that eludes his attempts to restrain it by growing, maddeningly, eternally, day after day, even though he's also preoccupied by the lesser animals fairly flaunting their unemployment—all this plus the fact that Eve develops close, nurturing relationships with flowers who spring up gladly at her touch. It's been explained to Adam that by the natural order of things in Eden, Eve is his "inferior," in both mind and body resembling God's image less than Adam does. But that teaching does not accord with what Adam himself *actually* experiences in her: which is not just her bodily "loveliness" but a quality of being in and knowing herself that is so "absolute," so "complete," that everything she says and does seems to him "wisest, virtuousest, discreetest, best" (8.550).

Eve too grapples with the discrepancy between the Adam she knows and the Adam she's been taught to revere, whose "manly grace / And wisdom" (4.490–91) are "Pre-eminent" (447) in the cosmic hierarchy of Eden. In the ordinary run of a day, Eve longs to be taken seriously by her husband, to know that Adam respects her enough not to get in the way of her desire to garden alone, for example, or to know that he trusts her "firm faith and love" (9.286), her honest contrition when events take an unexpectedly bad turn. "That thou shouldst my firmness . . . doubt," she says to him, when they're fighting about the danger they've learned lurks at the edges of the garden, "I expected not to hear" (9.281). Could there be a more poignant remark between wife and husband in this most emblematic of marriages? Long before Satan shows up, Adam is fretting less about disobedience to God than about the evil tempter disrupting his "conjugal love" (9.263), while Eve gets stuck on the equally terrible possibility of "another Eve" should she meet her maker in death (9.828). These are far from blissful newlyweds. They're jealous and they're insecure.

But in the mutual recrimination fest that is the initial aftermath of eating the apple, something emerges about what divorce *isn't*—just as Milton had intimated decades before—which is an escape hatch out of hardship. If we were supposed to bail at the first sign of trouble, Adam and Eve might've parted ways long before they get officially expelled. The lesson of *Paradise Lost* is that any marriage is a risk (even one supposedly ordained by God), since you never know when you hitch your team to that wagon what manner of mistakes will be made in the course of a life. Adam thinks he's "ruined" as soon as he finds out about the apple (9.906), but that's just what happens to the idealistic dream we once had of a perfect mate forged from the very stuff of ourselves—real life comes along and spoils it. The essence of love is whether or not you can keep talking long enough to find your way back inside each other, to the pith and mystery of self-with-other.

It isn't "faith in the beyond" that'll make us "less wretched," writes Nobel laureate Wislawa Szymborska, denouncing the supernatural, "but only doubt." We have to do our best *together* to feel less wretched inside.

IN THE FIRST few months after I got married, I would sometimes feel sorry for my husband that he was married to me, I was so sure I'd screw it up. I know that sounds piteous. I was Adam in my fretful repetitiveness that he wasn't behaving as I thought a spouse was supposed to, Eve in my surprise that he seemed unable to fathom my needs or moods. Downright Miltonic in my insistence that happiness requires *conversation / communication / communion / conversing*, as Adam reiterates in quick succession when he tells Raphael how lonely he was in the garden before Eve came along (8.418–32). But we can't live fully in the fear that we might do damage to others just by being ourselves.

In the final scene of Hemingway's *The Sun Also Rises*, Lady Brett, who's thirty-four and hasn't had kids, tells Jake that she isn't "going to be one of those bitches that ruins children" (243). She feels "rather damned good," she says, because of that fact; "deciding not to be a bitch" is "sort of what we have instead of God" (245). God "never worked very well" for her, she says. There's something desperately sad about consoling oneself over never having children—if having them was what you wanted—with the thought that you've thereby prevented yourself from being a bitch. But I get it. I was married at forty-four; that was supposed to mean I'd chosen thoughtfully, deliberately, that I'd grown up, learned something about myself, that my old demons might stop throwing their long shadows. But I was forever tamping him down; it was perilous, coming close to him; always a risk of getting lost, being subsumed. Well, Brett says, if we don't have faith of a religious sort as the framework for better behavior, we can at least decide not to be at our worst in the company of those we love. There is power in the act of not hurting someone.

How "miserable" it is, as Eve also says, another complicated wife full of desire and self-doubt, powerfully regretting actions whose outcome she had not been able to foresee, "To be to others cause of misery" (10.981–92). Maybe this is why Milton himself, apparently eager to enter "a grand Affair" with the daughter of one Dr. Davis, chose instead to patch things up with Mary Powell—"more inclinable to Reconciliation," in the words of nephew Edward, "than to perseverance in Anger and Revenge." If we can't believe in an immaterial being whose presence will never be guaranteed, we can still grab hold of kindness.

Which brings me back to Milton, defeated revolutionary under house arrest, blind author of *Paradise Lost,* and the sumptuousness of the poetry he imagined each night in the midst of all that pain. The sheer exuberant joy of words when your heart is breaking, and the consolation of being in the company of a man who carries writing on through shattering defeat because he feels our very capacity to exist is at stake in every line. Sure, I came to tears at least once in class, teaching Milton, because my marriage had come abruptly, absurdly, to a halt. But it wasn't just that private sadness. It was feeling like I'd crawled inside grandeur, with students I knew had their own reasons for needing ballast and hope. This is one of my versions of the ecstasy of faith—moments in class when I'd feel it deep in my bodily core, speaking Milton's truth, which had become our truth, about an urgently serious life you can only survive with others, hand in hand.

We don't have good words for the pleasures of learning. How, really, to describe that sensation of specifically intellectual excitement that happens when we talk about ideas, ones that matter vitally to us, in the company of others who are equally energized by the process? Milton's pedagogical program certainly didn't allow for that kind of sensuous electricity, but he lived it, I'm sure, and it's everywhere in *Paradise Lost,* embedded in his depiction of knowing-as-being-known: the charged, corporeal pleasure of a good long talk.

IT'S IN THE SMALLEST of textual moments—an image, an enjambment, a single word—that the epic registers just how hard we have to work to keep hold of what we know of ourselves, deep down, when we're instructed something different. When Eve tells Adam that she "oft remember[s]" the moment of her birth (4.449), *oft* denotes more than frequency; it is loaded with the implication of just how much delight Eve takes in the memory of her own company, before life got complicated by her man's vexed anxiety over edicts and decrees.

And when Adam says to Raphael, "well I understand . . . her the inferior, . . . yet when I approach / Her . . ." (8.540–41, 546–47), that *yet* works the opposite way. It's the dividing stile between the "dominion" Adam knows he's been granted over other creatures and the way his head spins when he comes close to Eve's astuteness and composure. *Yet, yet*—it's like he has to shake himself to comprehend the gap between heavenly pronouncements about his firstness and real life on earth with a woman whose sense of herself is stunningly whole. Into such seemingly insignificant words, the poem packs its refutation of grand paradigms. Even an adverb, the epic assures us, can undercut the imposition of doctrine on independent thinking. Put a few such lowly words together and they become a powerful army of movement and change. And that's where feeling is at its most authentic, its most urgent. At that level of startling potential.

I wonder sometimes if Milton would have been happier as a divorced seventeenth-century man, free to keep searching for the conversation that would satisfy him. (And if they had divorced, he and Mary Powell, would they have remained friends?) And is this what we should do, after all—keep up the search? I have no problem with divorce. Knowing a woman got divorced is like knowing she leases a car or has black hair or a pair of golden retrievers. It's *being divorced* that I can't quite face, which is why I'm still not, though we've lived apart for more than six years. We can give each other this, at least, however much we've failed to honor each other's dreams for a certain kind of happiness: forgiveness for being the flawed, inadequate humans we are. We can recognize the discrepancy between our expectations for a marriage and how it actually feels to be in it, inside those tiny, loaded words with which we try to communicate and all that space between them where we might constructively dismantle the rules. We can defy heavenly order and then *fall humble,* refuse to be wounded by the other's anger, ask for *commiseration* instead and remind ourselves that we love. We can live in the fullness of *ripe fruit*, dropping hand in hand into the world before us.

Those are all Milton's words, when he was into his third, last, and happiest marriage. And it's what I needed to believe, that fall, when trauma was having its slow, insidious way with me, when life had listed and lurched, and the only thing that really made sense was walking into class and getting down to poetic business. My students knew *something* was wrong (I told them as much). And I wasn't shy about letting them in on just how buoyed I felt by their eagerness for Milton—for his sense of purpose, his faith in language, his very difficulty, and the sense that everything was at stake, all the longing and hope and promise of the world, in every word.

4

MINDFUL MILTON

WHEN I WAS a little girl, I built a complex structure out of wooden blocks on the floor of my bedroom. It took me a long time, and it pleased me until it didn't, at which point I kicked the whole thing apart. Guilt and confusion immediately ensued—*what have I done?* When I told my mother, she asked the question out loud: "Why did you do that?" *Imperfection,* I thought even then, and know now. *Striving.* How unendurable it is to be oneself! If only I had understood, little meditator that I was, about sand mandalas, those exquisite, painstaking rituals of form and color that, in being created, mean nothing, and so are readily, also meaninglessly, destroyed. Not long ago I watched a televised group of Tibetan monks pour their tiny topography of crushed stone. It took them days and days to complete the riotously intricate design, and then they swept it all away again, reduced pattern and shape to a blurry swirl, and they were smiling while they did it, while I blinked back tears. It was almost more than I could stand, witnessing this—their riveted attention and their calm, their artistry and the deliberateness of their destruction of it. Almost more than I could *feel.*

But I did, nonetheless, feel it, and I recognized the sensation as akin to what I felt reading aloud the last lines of *Paradise Lost* in a meditation room at ten at night in a circle of fellow reciters. We had read every single word of all twelve books over ten hours, until the final moments when Adam and Eve take their way, hand in hand, into the fact of themselves. I choked up on those "natural tears they dropped" (12.645), that quick look back before they move forward toward an unknowable freedom. I didn't want it to end, the collective

40

sound of our voices in an atmosphere of poetry, the sense of a shared enterprise, the way we'd kept each other going through all those hours and all those lines. But Eden is not a lost thing in this moment; it is a means whereby the human couple carry on, a way they have come to know their own, and each other's, hardiness. I heard my voice; I sensed the presence of others; I felt the way Milton had mattered to me, an unlikely lifeline, in a period of terrible upheaval in my life. That we had achieved this thing together seemed in that moment wonderfully meaningful. That we had done this thing together meant nothing at all except in doing it.

We closed our books, walked out of the chapel into a rain-soaked parking lot, and took our separate ways.

I LEARNED TO MEDITATE when I was ten, in 1975. My father taught me. I had that square, yellow Seth Thomas clock to check my time and a mantra I devised for myself and good-enough posture to sit cross-legged against a wall for twenty minutes without pain in my back. For many years just thinking that mantra would slow my pulse and breathing and produce a warm calm. My mother gave birth to me from the slightly altered consciousness of a posthypnotic suggestion that eased her labor pains; I emerged from a self-soothing place, if I didn't stay long in one.

My parents were rationalists and hippies, one a psychologist, the other a future therapist. My father's heritage is Jewish, but he eschewed all that, as far as I knew as a kid; my mother's parents were middle-class Connecticut Presbyterians, origins she too got far away from as quickly as she could, and I remember from holidays in Fairfield only a few airless services punctuated by the brief reprieve of singing. There were times when I wished we were more Jewish. I knew the absence of religion in my father's fractured family had something to do with the death of relatives in the war and a residue of guilt and shame. But it wasn't God I wanted, back then—my own upbringing was so thoroughly unreligious that belief, I think, simply wasn't available to my imagination—but the ontology of something, the way a religion confers not just meaning but *being* along with the power and obscurity of its rituals. My atheist parents had Christmas trees and Jewish friends

who hosted seders where we kids would search for the hidden mat-
zoh and wait for Elijah, and something would register in me on those
occasions about the haroset and bitter parsley and eggs. Even now
I wish my memory could get beyond *Barukh ata Adonai Eloheinu,*
even if I can't reliably translate those words.

But the longing has never been for God. It is what the poet Philip
Larkin calls *hunger,* some need that compels even the staunchest
atheist (or rudest tourist) to "silence" in the "serious house" of worship. "[S]omeone will forever be surprising / A hunger in himself,"
Larkin writes in "Church Going," "to be more serious."

Seriousness is to Larkin—or this is how I understand it—what
"spirituality" seems to mean to people who are not, or maybe no longer, religious. Spirit without religion connotes a desire for something
"bigger," as people like to say, than the provinciality of self; it's believing in something apart from the institution of creed. But spirituality
used this casually has always struck me as a cop-out of sorts, a way of
hinting at religiosity without committing to it, satisfying that kind of
need without relinquishing some other secular status that religion is
presumed to compromise. Seriousness, though—this I have felt, as an
emotional expansiveness prompted by the artifacts of intensity: sculp-
ture, painting, poetry, music. By revelations of others' longing. "Auxiliaries," let's call them, which is the psychoanalyst Wilfred Bion's word,
the gorgeous ache of stretching-toward, to quell the crushing insignif-
icance we fear (and feel) at the core of ourselves. Seriousness as the
spare wood-smell of Quaker meeting at school when I was a girl; seriousness as that glimmer I get, of something possible, when we're told
to "seal the practice," palms against belly, at the end of a yoga class.
Closing my eyes from the pews of a candlelit local chapel in Florence
during an evening organ recital is a gesture of neither piety nor sacri-
lege. It is a longing for *depth.* An existential sadness that, in the cool silence of stone and vaulting proof of human artistry, might be soothed.

"Religion is a thin shell," writes Albert Goldbarth in *Dark Waves
and Light Matter,* "not an infrastructure" (6). Does this mean that its
protectiveness is scant, meriting suspicion when we deserve a stronger foundation? Or that we ask too much of it, building up its consolations without any attention to what's lacking—as well as what's
already robust—in ourselves? In the transitional moment in my for-

ties when I knew that talk therapy had run its course in me but meditation couldn't establish a hold, I wrestled (not quite Jacob) with old habits, trying at the same time to let go of some surety that an adjustment to my infrastructure was exactly what I needed. Think of how our metaphors define emotional well-being as *solidity*, how a literal need for shelter becomes a psychological expectation. Think of how we hammer and tinker away at ourselves, desperate for a nest, certain that wellness is synonymous with scaffolding.

Or call it editing, as we become ourselves in the stories we tell. And then call that *chatter*, the incessant nattering of a mind unable to still itself. The solace of prayer is not just faith that some more puissant being will care for us; it's in talking to an interlocutor. If we're deaf, maybe we sign it. However the telling, so it seems, thereby we take ownership and so control; we lessen the beast by reducing it to words we can manipulate. How many political movements have galvanized our desire to live "out loud," our trust in reclaiming a "voice"? It's one way of explaining why therapy works, as my father has told me; shame loves the shadows, and utterance defangs it.

I've spent a lot of time digging at myself, diligent archaeologist, years on the couch searching for the key to my immutable self, cultivating the story, wanting to believe in something like *pith*, an essential core of identity whose convolutions I could disentangle by talking enough—by *working through*. Originary trauma—it's seductive, that Freudian idea, the golden-egg promise of a trauma that, in being revealed, is just as soon repaired. But even if it's true (and aren't we infinitely messier than that?), even if we can say, *this happened to me, I was badly used, there wasn't enough love to go around,* that telling will never be enough; knowing is not the same as freeing. Knowing, in fact, leads as often to repetition as it does to change, as we pack ourselves into the story we then lug forever through space and time— the *idea* of ourselves—like spinner suitcases with wonky wheels. The Buddhist metaphor is a house, a construct we erect to shield ourselves from hurt; we decorate just so, illuminate with light, all the while ignoring completely the sun-filled wildflower meadow our little edifice is smack in the middle of. Funny, when I think of it, how much money I've spent on wildflower seeds that will never grow in the shady, acidic soil of my pine-treed yard.

So here I am in a tangle of metaphor, saying only by likening in an endless string of *this* as *that*, bringing me no closer to some essence of self but only to third terms my figures of speech have created. If we can talk ourselves into solidity, we also analogize ourselves right out of existence.

To say is not inevitably to change. Perhaps it is to *stay*.

WHEN MILTON'S SATAN finds out that he is not, after all, a self-begotten being but instead a creation of God—and not even that but "the work / Of secondary hands, by task transferred / From Father to his Son" (5.853–55)—he makes one of the funniest remarks in all of *Paradise Lost:* "Strange point and new!" (855). There's something dopey about it (Satan as Scooby-Doo—*huh?*), but it's also character-istically arrogant. The fallen angel is a proper revolutionary in his objection to bowing and scraping before a tyrannical lord, to an eter-nity of "warbled hymns" and "Forced hallelujahs" (2.242–43). But he misses entirely the distinction between being self-begotten and self-authored, between subjection and subjectivity. In his adamant refusal of any obligation to another, his single-minded focus on getting back at the Father he feels abandoned by and the other son who has re-placed him, he also deprives himself of any possibility of change. It's hard to give free rein to creativity when you're hell-bent on avenging all the egregious wrongs that have been done to you. Satan is, ulti-mately, and for all his seductive speechifying in the first two books of the epic, stuck in the binary opposition of good and evil and re-markably unimaginative for such a rousing rhetorician. Satan does not adjust, adapt, revise, or reconsider. He is in need, one might say, of a good therapist. As one of my students once seriously remarked, he needs to *let it go*.

Adam and Eve, by contrast, are defined by their capacity to deter-mine their own paths. Where Satan is stuck in the past, gnawing and stewing on his family-of-origin trauma, the human pair are famously "authors to themselves in all" (3.122), and they liberate themselves from the stagnations and coercions of the Eden Milton composes for them because they stay in creative motion. They choose, they fail, they repair, they wander, they choose again. They make it up as they go along. Call it *practice*, as we say of meditation—and religion, too, as well as the arts—trying to make a habit of it, working on getting it less wrong, putting it *into* practice. It's important that Milton writes it this way: Satan stuck in the past, God and archangels trying to focus Adam and Eve on the "happy end" yet to come (in fact far in a future the first humans can't know [12.605]), and Adam and Eve themselves in mindful, day-by-day consciousness. It's not that the human pair don't fret or perseverate or hurt each other (they do), but that in being alert to how they *actually* feel, to the evidence of their own experience, they resist the grander narratives of who they're supposed to be, the stultifying pressure of literalizing a paradigm.

By the time I was teaching Milton in that aggrieved fall of 2015, twenty-five years into my career, I'd started thinking of the poet as a good Buddhist. It's an absurd clash of theologies, I know, which ultimately serves my own desire for continuity—maybe what the painter René Magritte used to call affinities—more than anyone's understanding of Milton. I don't say much about this in class. It's just that Milton's plea to his readers to eschew complacency, in text after text, resonates in me like the precept that getting caught up in story prevents us from being able to transform. There's no evidence that Milton, on the brink of eighteenth-century Enlightenment philosophy, had any connection to Eastern spiritual practice. But maybe he's been, paradoxically and nonetheless, my bridge between a lifetime of worry and compulsive self-narration (what Buddhism calls *samsara*, neurotic existence), and *shamatha*, or calm abiding. A restless, nervous thinker who writes in his Eve a steady, mindful awareness, noticing without evaluating, when she interacts with the stuff of her garden, and with herself. A Christian hermeneuticist who gives us prelapsarian sex and the pleasures—no, the existential *foundation*—of an embodied life, our most intensive psychical experiences inextricable from our corporeal selves. A daring heretical man who, setting aside the particular limitations of the character Satan, makes hell a mutable category subject to imaginative revision, a *heaven*, even, in the poem's most oft-quoted reversal (1.255).

Or to put this all a little differently, a poet who can take the old story of human failure, with its graphic accounting of life's miserable events—epic loss, betrayal, violence, and fear—and remind us of the quiet kindnesses we still pay each other. The possibility of love told not in happy endings but in radical not-knowing. The consolations of master paradigms refused; resilience, patience, gentleness embraced. "The mind is its own place," Satan tells his rebel compatriots (1.254), just before they ensnare themselves in elaborate scenarios of revenge, clinging not to the possibility of transformation but to the selves they've always been. Because just there, at that enjambment on "and in itself . . . ," in the white space that blooms marvelously at the end of a line, they *could* make a different turn: not backward into the frozen binaries of heaven and hell, acquiescence and war, but outward to the adventure of uncertainty. For to say *I'm in hell* is to say *I'm in life*, fragile, painful, also boring existence. But I might choose neither to defend nor hide.

Doctrine makes Adam and Eve's trespass the woe of all humanity. Mindfully embodied compassion makes it the occasion of renewed understanding. That's how they find their way back to each other through the bitter "mutual accusation" (9.1187) of guilt-ridden post-apple bad-sex heartache. Adam and Eve have their own version of the hellish council when they try, desperate with grief and remorse, to decide what to do about the anguish they've wrought. Childlessness, maybe, or suicide. Anything to quell that certainty of having wrecked the best thing that ever happened. In the end they decide "a long day's dying" (10.964) is just another word for life. They hold hands and they walk.

KIERKEGAARD TELLS US THAT the most painful state of being is remembering a future we'll never have. I grasp this in the sense of mourning my daydreams in a perpetual state of yearning. And, less opaquely, in the sense of lying awake in the silent middle of night coping with a solitariness I did not know was going to define my fifties. That is the madness of marriage come asunder, the loss of a future, and the selves we thought we could be within the surety of it. For years after the split—still, now, in the very moment of typing this sentence— I cannot quite reconcile myself to the loss of the plans we had, of the version of myself I was becoming within the various narratives of *married, not single, not about to grow older* (read, demented, as this is my genetic legacy) *terrified and alone.* Even if I can say, assuredly, that I am happier now, on my own. Which means the story I'm telling is the memoir of a future I can't relinquish. Which means the future is a compulsive rehearsal of something that obtained in the past.

What made it all the more wrenching, the collapse of it, was that I had married *consciously.* One afternoon, before we'd moved in together, I was vacuuming the bedroom rug and thinking that he made me want to be a better person. I'd never *felt* a cliché that way, as that kind of crystal-clear sensory experience, and there was something of the visionary in it. It conferred a legitimacy on the thing we were doing. It was . . . *serious.* He had character, integrity; I would rise above the pettiness of my neurotic complaints and find true joy. Oh, I'd been reading about mindfulness for a while by then; I was done with talk therapy and its excavations of childhood; I would burst forth into my better self unencumbered by obsession with imperfections (mine?— surely—as well as his) and we would burnish a love together. In the event, it's obvious, the harder I tried, the more critical I grew of my own criticalness, the less I was actually practicing it, the Buddhism I pretended to grasp.

Grasping, of course, is what keeps us stuck. Like starving wraiths from the realm of the Hungry Ghosts (one of six on the Wheel of Life), wracked with a hunger that every attempt to satiate merely worsens. Exactly like the fallen angels in *Paradise Lost.* Unaware that the emptiness we dread in ourselves need not be proof of a shameful brokenness we must do what we can to shield, but instead, if we could quiet the noise long enough to tune into it, might simply be felt as the state of no-self, beautiful in its amplitude.

When the rebel angels slither up to that fateful tree, "fondly thinking to allay / Their appetite," their mouths fill up with "bitter ashes" instead of fruit (10.~565), and they're destined to keep craving for all eternity. Adam and Eve have long since decided that true love means we stop asking to be fed.

IN A CLASS I once taught called "Mindfulness and Memoir," I tried to get authorial intention to collide with Buddhist demolition. I wanted to know if we could inhabit mindfulness on the page without setting off in search of it, since the forward-motion of questing defeats the very notion of presence. What is called *bare attention*, moment-to-moment awareness of our changing perceptions, simply being a witness to what is now—could we *write* that? And would it amount to something more interesting than page after page of random notation? ("Breathing in, breathing out . . . noticing . . . noticing . . . God, this is boring . . . not judging . . . breathing again . . ."—I read whole student pages of that.) Could we liberate memoir from its genre-defining reflectiveness and strong persona?

We read a resoundingly linear memoir by a Buddhist nun, whip-smart ironic essays by the Thai American writer Ira Sukrungruang about being Buddhist as a kid on Chicago's South Side, books about secular Buddhism, Pico Iyer on stillness, a Buddhist meditation in which the artificial house of self is reduced to rubble, and pain as a felt, bodily experience is not narrated in terms of suffering. We were *immersing*. Sometimes we meditated together in class. I asked us (because I was writing along with them) to find new metaphors for identity, to shuck the old tropes of *that* person, *that* memory, *that* sequence of self's causation. I asked us to witness, not reify; to explore "I" as a habit, not an essence. Midway through, I let us rail and rage, cling to the old tales, resist change, indulge every familiar idea we'd ever had about who we are, plagiarize ourselves. Then I set us free all over again, asked us to breathe and associate, manipulate words as constitutive, not representative, of selves that had never existed in time or space, just one iteration of self that might suddenly dissipate—self-life-writing as wisps of cloud the Buddhists liken to momentary thinking across the wide sky of consciousness, its deeper blue.

And at the end of all that, in the week before every one of them would graduate from college and go forth into versions of themselves they had surely not quit fretting about however much we tried not to rehash the past or idealize the future—well, there we all were, sitting in a pub around pitchers of beer, narrating the hell out of exactly who we'd always been.

IF MEMORY IS NOT documentary retrieval but always an act of narrating past event (as the neuroscientists tell us), then past and future exist purely in the grievances of story—or in story as a mode of grieving, by which I mean both mourning and complaint. Or: the future has already happened, formed by our urgent need to repair the past, such that memoir/history and fantasy/future are one and the same, hope no different from an elastic memory. To put this differently again: a "memoir of a future"—which is the title of Bion's posthumously published 678-page tome—has something to do with "consolidating the system to prevent the intrusion of yet another thought" (265). Less densely: we work hard to barricade our fragile psyches against each other—especially another person's *ideas*, or even the very *idea* of each other, precisely because we feel so sure (and so scared) that our very futures depend on each other for the fulfillment of our fantasies, our longings, our plans. Psychical circularity is such that we live into a future that is not so much predetermined by the past as it is experienced as an endless series of reminiscences we luxuriate in, daydreaming our way into better, brighter versions of existence, worrying the suspicion that we're not, can't possibly be, *always already alright*.

Auxiliaries (I invoke them above) is Bion's word for art, which concentrates meaning in the way a therapeutic encounter can also concentrate our understanding of ourselves. On the same page of Bion's text (I opened to it randomly), Milton appears as an example of a writer who seems to grasp, in the epic attempt that is *Paradise Lost,* that "he must do for himself in loneliness and despair" (333). Milton wrote that poem from house arrest in a mood of profound existential uncertainty. A revolution had failed, his youthful sense of being on the right side of history had been seriously rattled, and his work turned from topical political controversy in prose to a vatic, poetic mode of what-comes-next; maybe writing his nation into its future could assuage the disappointment of having failed the promise of the present.

But Bion makes the effect of reading *Paradise Lost* a here-and-now matter of availability, invoking the epic in the same breath as what he calls the "*minimum* conditions" of analyst and analysand "at the same time and in the same place . . . consciously discern[ing] facts" (his italics). I read that mouthful this way: when analysis is at its most mindful, both parties are fully present to the process, wholly engaged with each other as presences in the room, breathing and being. This aligns reading with psychoanalysis as intimate encounters with something outside ourselves through which we (re)discover ourselves. *Paradise Lost* is the kind of poem whose courageous faith in human love and human creativity can embolden us to rethink every piety we've ever learned. It insists that intimacy can't substitute for solitude— there are times, as when Eve demands to garden alone, when someone else will just get in our way—but it also shouldn't compel us *into* solitude; if it does, then there's trouble in Paradise indeed. All this makes "doing for" yourself in your worst, lonely moments seem like not so insurmountable a thing, since aloneness for Milton simply means knowing who you are at your core.

When a certain celebrity told a recent graduating class of my college to "find their truth," a student who'd taken Milton with me (she of the unruly hair and wild intelligence) emailed the next day to enthuse of said celeb, "she's a Miltonist!" Yes: even in the watered-down popularized *you do you* of a commencement speech we might discern Milton's heretical individuality, his refusal to acquiesce to conventional norms and institutional laws, his insistence on you and only you at the crossroads of choice every minute of every day. But there's a world of difference between that easy promise of a stable self we need only calm down and access, and Milton's brand of truth, which is less a thing than a process, rendered variously in one political tract as a branching tree, a streaming fountain, human digestion, the discrete but connected stones of a wall, and the scattered but retrievable body parts of Osiris. In other words, particles in a contiguous whole. Unlikes shoved up against each other. Transitory moments of arrival. All of it requiring moment-to-moment attention, full-*body* attention, in fact—the whole of our touching, eating, loving, talking, seeing, feeling selves, headlong and serious, in deep-down meditative company with others.

Which might mean the celebrity was saying a legitimately mindful thing (even in seeming to promise material success if we follow our passion—she herself is, after all, very, very rich), if only in assuring us that we have nothing to compensate for, no wrongness to mend except perhaps to say, *I did wrong by you,* and *I'm sorry.* And my student was right, too, about the Miltonism of that, given the poet's disdain for ideologies of coercion and fawning obedience before the

arbiters of correctness. Adam and Eve are at their best in this way
when at their worst, in the angry aftermath of trespass, when the cru-
cial act that shifts the tide of history is not prayer but a man and a
woman asking each other's forgiveness, *tending* each other, we might
say, in the here.

In the moments before he eats the apple, Adam says to Eve, "past
who can recall, or done undo?" It's a funny thing to think—*what's
done is done*—before you've even done it, but no sense perseverating.
"[L]ead on," as Eve will later say (12.614): life awaits. Not even "God
omnipotent" (9.926-27) can unwill the moment-to-moment facts of
time, and choice, and being.

MY HUSBAND, WHO once scoffed at the Buddhist teaching that
life is suffering, now meditates every day. He's taken to wearing two
bands of pea-sized beads around one wrist to call him to the practice.
Like a rosary, I said when I noticed these mala bracelets, thinking of
his Catholic boyhood, long left behind, but also wondering, I'll admit, who gave him those bracelets. Would he tell me if I asked? (The
wounds heal, the wounds are always there.) Neither of us is religiously
Buddhist, but he says it organizes the mind, softens the anxiety. This
is a man who will still deny he feels fear, even when I press him to tell
me why we haven't gotten divorced. About the meditating, I admire
his tenacity.

One morning, a few years separated by then, determined to make
good on my own intentions, I lay back in bed and opened my shoulders in a restorative pose my therapist had taught me as the embodied
form of peaceful retreat. I felt the old sadness *immediately,* a swell of
bereftness as if without story I am inherently a vessel of loss, which
is to say nothing but traces and impressions. Immediately it asserted
itself, the dog-eared narcissism of complaint. And then I thought,
must I? Is *this* the fundamental me? Story is revisable by definition.
Even a rutted laneway can be repaved. (I've never said "laneway" before, though I like the quaint sound of it. It's the Canadian term for
driveway. He influences still.) The world is so much bigger than these
private tales. If compassion on the grand scale seems too abstract—if

it inspires guilt more than fellow feeling—we can nonetheless bore ourselves into action. I don't mean *drill* like boring into something with purposive force. I mean *weary* yourself out of yourself.

It was a revelation to me in that moment (if I can use that loaded word) to understand in some bodily way the Buddhist credo that we are not our thoughts. I felt sadness lift off me like evaporating fog. I got up from the bed, walked into the day somehow lighter, my spirits (by which I will always mean mood) perceptibly lifted. It was strange. Liberating, you might say. And new.

5

PAPER CRANES

FOR MONTHS AFTER my husband and I separated, I did not open a book. This presented a peculiar problem for a college professor of English. Or: I would open a book, stare without understanding at the words, close it again. I knew people for whom books of poetry had offered solace in times of shattering grief; I looked at poems as if they were maps of foreign countries I'd never heard of, a badly translated set of instructions for reassembling an appliance that had never worked in the first place. At last, one night, I read Rilke's *Letters to a Young Poet* in its entirety, leaning forward on the couch to propel my searching for some kind of revelation. I had not remembered how much of that slim volume concerns the agonies of solitude and Rilke's faith in a future in which women might redefine the very contours of love.

"Most experiences are unsayable," writes Rilke to his correspondent Franz Kappus; "they happen in a space that no word has ever entered" (4). This is why, after my husband and I separated, I watched the same TV episodes obsessively, over and over, until I could recite the dialogue at the same time that I could not for the life of me remember their plots. Narrative had stopped making sense. Shape as episteme had no logic. I could not bear the presence of my wedding dresses hanging like deflated mannequins in bags in the closet and within the first two months produced forty single-spaced pages that hyperventilated hysterically around the same three or four points.

Moments after I discovered my husband's affair, I staggered to a hospital waiting room for overwrought family members, his phone in my hand, and copied love language not to me on the back of a piece of paper on which I had typed up all the medications he was on: two sides of a now-incomprehensible story. At some point, I don't know how, I walked away from him altogether, sat down opposite a bank of elevators, and burst into tears. When I heard a woman say, "I'm so sorry for whatever you're going through," I knew she'd assumed my loved one just got a death sentence. In a sense, I thought, we had. My husband had lived through heart surgery; he would survive having his gall bladder removed. He would live.

But we had lost the shape of things altogether.

RELATIONSHIP, ALIBI, LOVE-NOTE, worry, prayer: these are forms, genres, with typical modes of getting started, accumulating information, making themselves coherent. We depend on their conventions to know what comes next, what to expect, which is why we flounder so awkwardly when things go awry—when form and content no longer coincide. Milton the iconoclast (literally, "image or idol breaker") thoroughly understood the power as well as the danger of forms. He was a talented musician, after all, a superior rhetorician and speechifier, and a poet who opens his major work with a justification of shucking the rhyme that had characterized epics before his ("rhyme," he declared, "is no necessary adjunct of true poetry"). In his October 1649 pamphlet *Eikonoklastes,* Milton took up an overtly formbusting politics, dismantling the portrait of Charles I as a sainted martyr that had been circulating throughout England and on the continent that year in the posthumously published *Eikon Basilike* (Image of the king), with its frontispiece engraving of Charles kneeling beneath beams of celestial light. Here Milton shatters such idols as liturgical form and rote prayers, two components of the English church under Charles that he found especially objectionable. This is why Adam and Eve, decades later, "observ[e]" no "rites," but instead pray freely under the "open sky," the expression of devotion that "God likes best" (4.736–78).

The forms things take, then, as a measure of their meaning, their value, their impact on their audience. Our ideas about coupledom have everything to do with shape in this sense, since how two people inhabit its framework is so bound up with the rituals associated with it and its social, legal, religious import—its role in the myriad structures by which a culture defines itself. In making a bid for marriage as a function of psychological attunement and the freewheeling unpredictability of conversation, heretical Milton wasn't just smashing the false idol of men's interpretations of the theological impediment to divorce. He was coaxing his audience to reorient their attitudes toward emotion—love, anger, loneliness, desire, boredom, ambition. To say that there's a proper way to "do" anything, including our own feelings, is to obscure the pressure of *narrative:* the organizing, dominant metapatterns by which we live.

In his *Commonplace Book,* notes on his readings over thirty years or more, Milton writes, in a section headed "Of Divorce," "After a husband's absence for five years, if it is uncertain where he is, the right is granted to the wife to marry another" (407). I read this (full disclosure: for the first time) when my own husband had been absent nearly five years. Oh, I know where he "is" (he just left my house, taking Jack to PetSmart for his every-three-weeks nail clip). But we can be unsure of a person's relative location in so many ways. Doesn't it take seven years to declare a missing person dead? I can't imagine the incoherence of that sort of empty space. Once, early on in the separation, my husband told me he was going to Canada for a weekend, but when I texted one of his sisters to ask when he'd left to come home, she said he hadn't been at all. I forgot how big a country it is, that long stretch of border, while I messaged friends of his I barely knew and tried to decide I was overreacting while my mind conjured grungy motel rooms he might be in—whether for pleasure or in despair. When at last he emerged, explained he'd been with other friends, in a different city, not his hometown, I leaned all the way in to believing him. Story is how we fill the hollows of fear. Story is defensive palisade.

It's easy to lose track of the fact that the central four books of *Paradise Lost* are essentially conversation, in which the archangel Raphael describes for the human pair the cosmic beginnings of their existence: the war in heaven and creation of the world. In fact *Paradise Lost* proceeds almost entirely through storytelling. Book 3 is devoted to God and the Son articulating different versions of what's to come. Adam and Eve, too, spend their time together relating their perspectives on life and exercising their fledgling capacities for philosophical debate. Later the archangel Michael takes over, displaying before Adam the scope of human history. These stories have arcs we understand—conflict and denouement—with known heroes and villains. What makes them interesting is not the suspense of an unknown ending; it's more about watching Milton manipulate predetermined shapes. He takes what we think we know and reforms it toward exhilarating surprise.

I LEARNED HOW TO FOLD origami cranes after a trip to Hiroshima, where garlands of brightly colored cranes are piled at the base of monuments to symbolize peace and hope. I brought home thick packets of origami paper—two-inch squares of gilded reds and blues, pinks and greens—and folded tiny cranes with a strange determination to produce a string of a thousand before the year was up, because according to legend, anyone who folds a thousand cranes will be granted one wish. I confess I faltered after a hundred or less, but I have them still, a purple glass bowl of baby cranes afloat on the living room table, in recognition of courage, a beauty in the face of devastation, that I had never witnessed before. Something about that kind of belief I wanted—not just to preserve, but to imitate.

Perhaps that's why, a decade later, planning for my marriage to a man who would one day break my heart, I started folding cranes again. Bigger ones this time, in raucous animal prints and metallics and pastel diamond squares and a crayon palette of solid color. I cannot say where the impulse came from, only that it struck me with a curious inevitability, an obviousness, as if cranes had been nesting in my imagination, ready to bloom, year after year. I wanted them as table decorations along with fresh-cut flowers we would arrange ourselves. Symbols of fidelity, some say, because cranes mate for life, and their lives (as bird lives go) are relatively long.

At first I thought I'd fold as many cranes as we expected guests at the wedding, but the process of making them—choosing the paper, creasing the seams with my fingernail, breathing a little air into the pocket that would become their bodies—was too captivating to relinquish after only so few. I folded crane after crane, one hundred, two hundred, a wicker basket full of them and then more than the basket could hold, until the cats could not be stopped from stalking their paper prey, and I had to store the overflowing hundreds of cranes on a shelf high in a closet. Even now I do not know quite what they meant, only that every crane whose tail I stretched, whose head I formed, seemed a demonstration of will; delicate, miniature monuments to grace. Just like a marriage, according to tradition. An effort of perseverance, of time and trust.

And yet it surprises me, the seriousness with which the cranes were watched over on the day I got married. One of my sisters lay cloth napkins over them on their tables so they wouldn't blow away in the wind. Photographs were taken of them by every friend who documented the event. And several of them ended up at others' houses, party favors we hadn't intended. When I came upon them at dinner parties months after the fact, unexpected gaggles I made myself of color and shape, it was as if something of the joy of that day had literally taken flight.

A string of a thousand cranes is called a *senbazuru*. When the Chinese first brought origami to Japan, paper was expensive and the art could only be practiced by the rich. Colors and shapes took on special meaning, indicating family name and status, perhaps even emotion. Some say the intricacy of paper-folding made it an especially useful vehicle for passing love notes, because it is difficult to refold a crane without leaving behind the traces of your interception. Discovery would be swift.

For many years there were no written instructions for origami; the technique was passed from generation to generation by practitioners of the art, by demonstration, by apprenticeship and a desire to perfect the craft. The first written guide appeared in the late 1700s: *How to Fold 1,000 Cranes*. According to legend, folding a thousand cranes would ensure the granting of your greatest desire. Any diligent reader could make a wish come true, because only the most persistent would endure. Cranes had long been associated with nobility and respect. The Chinese believed them to have the dignity of a gentleman and a privileged status as messengers to the ancient immortals. To be described as "a figure extolled by the crane" was high praise indeed. To be likened to a crane was to be honored as "exceptionally honest and morally upright."

Do I need to tell you about how I rifled through my husband's things, desperate for evidence of a love he had not shared with me? A letter, a card, anything to document—in a form I could take hold of—the unimaginable thing that had made my life unrecognizable? Should I say that the day after I found out my husband was having an affair, I went to the hospital with a Valentine's Day card I'd given him in sweeter, hopeful times, found stored in a sock drawer, and tore it in front of him into ragged pieces that fluttered to the tray-table next to the incentive spirometer and a plastic jug of water, as he looked on with an expression on his face I thought even at the time was mournfully beautiful, lying in a hospital bed in a green gown that offset the cornflower blue of his eyes?

In *Paradise Lost*, Milton includes the "prudent Crane" (7.430) in his list of birds whose wisdom and intelligence he praises as much as he revels in the beauty of their plumage or their song. Prudence connotes discretion. Prudence connotes restraint.

A LONG TIME AGO, when I was struggling to comprehend my own unhappiness, my mother sent me a card that said, "Into every life, a little crane must fall." A tiny stick-pin crane was taped inside, a green-and-blue badge of courage I could wear out into the world.

I found the stick-pin crane many years later, at the bottom of a box, as I made space in a closet of boxes for my new husband's things, artifact of a time in my life when I often felt lonely and adrift. When I was folding origami cranes ahead of our wedding, I hadn't known—or hadn't remembered—this presence in my life of cranes as an icon of humor and solace. And something else, too, about what befalls a life, what we can ask of each other by way of comfort when circumstances elude our ability to understand or to change.

Into every life a little crane must fall. What did it mean, the crane that rhymed with rain, that should have been but wasn't rain? Do we not grow up insistently ourselves, if only because it never occurs to us we could be anything but? Don't we hone the people we become within the stories of our lives, in the childhood memories we polish to a gleaming luster of (for example) melancholic sadness? We're clay figurines taking shape under our own wet hands, like a worked and reworked paragraph. I say this because I've been talking about identity in terms of story. Because even the interruption of forward movement by the catastrophic—*into every life*—can feel plotted, even preordained. Because watershed moments from which *what happened next* can seem to cascade with purposiveness and force.

For a time, I told a causal story of marrying my husband because my father got badly injured by a horse and our lives altered in an instant. It was a wet morning in the Texas hills, the Sunday after Thanksgiving. My father went out to feed his four horses, entering the paddock with buckets of oats and flakes of hay, in cowboy boots well scuffed at the heel and slick as ice on muddy ground. The rest is conjecture. He managed to come in from the yard through a rear door to the master bathroom, where my stepmother found him. His right cheekbone was smashed, and a deep, bleeding cut extended from just below his eyelashes to the hairline above his right ear. Somehow the injury had missed his eye, and he was conscious. *I did something stupid,* he said. Only later did anyone understand how dangerous a habit he'd formed in feeding the horses from within the paddock where the horses would jostle for dominance, chasing each other away from the buckets of feed. It seems my father, unsteady on his feet in the smooth boots on slippery mud, got in the middle of—was knocked down by one of—those massive bodies, and hit his head on a rock. Or, struggling to right himself, was clipped in the face by a hoof, ten pounds of pure steel nailed in place and swinging like a miniature wrecking ball.

The day my father fell down in the mud, I hadn't spoken to him for an entire year. Only under this extremity of condition, my heart beating wildly, did I finally pick up the phone. *I'm so sorry, I did a stupid thing,* he said from a stretcher, awaiting surgery in the ER, where they wouldn't give him anything for the pain because you don't give narcotics to a man with head injury. *I love you,* I said, and waited by the phone when he went into surgery to reconstruct his face, and I spoke to him the day after that, and again the next, and every day for six months at least. My father fell down in the mud, got clipped by a lazy hoof and came up from the ground with a face in pieces. Overnight I unlearned years of knowing myself as an angry daughter. A few days later, I emailed my future husband to apologize for a temporary rift we were in. My father's accident—the reorganization of priorities it initiated, of bones, flesh, family, alignments of desire and love—made it seem absurd to hold onto trivial preferences and pet peeves.

For several years into my marriage, I felt all this as a nearly mystical convergence of events that heralded my new beginning. My father getting hurt was such an obvious lesson in life's fragility (just as Jack's little escapade, a decade on, would be such an obvious reminder of unpredictable loss). Dad's bones knitting together, the hairline scar that would be visible below his eye for a long time to come, were ready metaphors for opportunity, renewal, even beauty, like the Japanese art of *kintsugi*, where pottery is deliberately broken and then mended with gold-dusted lacquer. I thought the experience of rapprochement with Dad had taught me how to let go of old resentments and a powerful need for relationships to proceed *just so*. My husband-to-be impressed me as someone who had achieved his own share of introspective awareness. Together we would fashion a love defined by generosity and tolerance. Love could be *simple*. Reinvention was possible.

The January after my husband and I separated, I went to Texas for a conference. I hadn't seen much of my father in the decade since he got hurt by a horse, his beloved Tennessee walker of the sluggish hooves, because after that initial reconciling, we slid naturally back toward distance and our lackadaisical ways about staying in touch. But I felt no heat around that anymore. Dad would have plenty to say about my situation, including, late into one night, after too much booze, *He's a lovable rogue! Take him back!* But the first night, he just sat quietly with me as I cried at his kitchen table. My father's no stranger to trauma. He was holding my hand, and I remember being surprised at how soft his skin was, despite all the work he does in the barn, hefting bales of hay and wiggling fingers deep in the ears of his horses, which he claims they like. He sat with me a long time, my hand in his hand, murmuring *yes, yes.*

PARTING, ACCORDING TO Emily Dickinson, who loved her sister-in-law with a trembling intensity, is "all we need of hell."

Edward Phillips tells us, in his biography of the famous uncle, that when Mary Powell failed to return to London after a summer sojourn by the agreed-upon date of Michaelmas, at the end of September, Milton "sent for her by Letter; and receiving no answer, sent several other Letters, which were also unanswered; so that at last he dispatch'd down a Foot-Messenger with a Letter, desiring her return; but the Messenger came back not only without an answer, at least a satisfactory one, but . . . reported that he was dismissed with some sort of Contempt" (64–65). Did he fold them ever more frantically, those squares of paper, lined with his ink? I imagine the third, the fourth, the increasing sense of confusion and rage. Where *was* she? He began to fear an inevitable and horrid outcome, forced to stay married to a person who'd rejected him so outrageously. Such an inexplicable interruption to the anticipated trajectory of their lives! Milton got quickly to work on the first of his divorce tracts, fashioning a whole polemic out of private humiliation (how can we *not* read that document autobiographically?), taking on the edifices of church and state, smashing the whole house down.

Oru: to fold. *Kami:* paper. Any origami object will bear the marks of its making: creases down the centers of a wing, through the middle of a head or a tail, like the scars of birth, finger whorls of how it began in two dimensions. The December after my July wedding, I sent crane ornaments to the friends who'd helped us achieve that beautiful day. I wanted them to believe, when they saw their birds swinging there, in a window over a sink, on a Christmas tree, from a filament of fishing line strung from the ceiling, that into every life enchantment might fall. How many still dangle there, origins unremembered—or, in solidarity with me, in protest against an apparently singular act that rent my union, got crumpled at the bottom of a recycling bin? In a plastic bin beneath the guest bed, I still have the piece of paper on which I copied down the texts I read as it dawned on me I was living a spectacular untruth. I also have the marriage vows we wrote, and every card he gave to me that I didn't tear to shreds. We hold onto the tangible as long as we can. We make these arbitrary shapes the container of our hopes.

When the future I'd imagined with my husband collapsed in on itself, I held fast to certain continuities, to friendship and sisterhood, to my father and the scar that was his broken face, to the faint outlines of folds on scraps of paper held out to me in dreams in which all the colors were inside out and torqued two degrees to the left on the color wheel, saying, *mountain folds back, valley folds forward.* Flat expanse of color and pattern shaped to hold abstractions—like forgiveness, like love—by my own hands. But I no longer remember how to fold a crane without instructions, how to breathe life into a square-shaped space formed only by the edges of a thing.

6

UMBRIAN HOLIDAY

I WAS EXPLAINING to a few people over dinner that, in my absence, my animals and house were being looked after by my husband. I was at a conference in Italy, and I'd been legally separated for four years. From the corner of my eye I caught the man sitting next me, someone I'd known for thirty years, shake his head. Almost imperceptibly, but it registered.

Separated people ought to get divorced already. Divorced people should not remain friends.

I feel sure I've heard of couples who stay separated and never divorce the way you remember slights from fifth grade or a fight you won with someone else's cousin at a distant Thanksgiving—dimly, but with righteous certitude.

And the irony of that situation in Italy is that the man next to me, inclining his grayed head in what I feared was disapproval, had been a father figure to me for a long time. His son is the ex who sent me that Hemingway quote about happiness; we met in our twenties, and were together for twelve years. I was in Italy with both of them, at an artists' and writers' conference. Because the son and I have remained good friends. It was the son who had invited me along.

We have no ready words for such relationships, because we can't really understand them, maybe don't fully endorse them. Exes who feel like family and spouses who've betrayed you past the brink of trust but still house-sit when you go on vacation, to mow the lawn and care for the dog you rescued together from its flea-ridden state at a local pet adoption fair. Last spring I heard someone refer to her ex as her "was-band," and I tried that out for a while, liking its sly rhyme, the way it seemed perfectly to capture the role of a man who techni-cally is but is not my husband. The problem with "was-band," though, was that I kept having to define it. Which meant also trying to define the way I love a person, cannot completely detach from a person, even though I was so hurt by him, and am glad we're not together anymore. What do you call a legal husband you have no romantic feelings for? "Friendship" seems too small a word for a bond once specifically de-fined as more than that. (Milton-the-divorcer scoffed at the institu-tions of marriage *and* friendship as narrow constraints on true mutu-ality.) How do we keep loving when we've fallen out of love?

Shouldn't we try?

"[G]OING TO ANOTHER country doesn't make any difference," says Jake to Robert in Hemingway's *The Sun Also Rises*, when his friend threatens to ditch Paris for South America. "You can't get away from yourself by moving from one place to another." It's a truism by now, that we carry ourselves with us wherever we go. ("You take your brain," as a recent alum texted me from Belgrade.) But there's also the oppo-site truism of travel—that going to another country will make all the difference in the world when we're soul-sick where we are. Unmoored from the restraints of home, we become freer, fuller, even better ver-sions of who we are. We don't just enjoy being there, we actually enjoy being *ourselves*.

In the spring of 2015, I spent three weeks in Florence, where my husband had once worked as an executive for General Electric. I was due to take over as chair of my department on the first of June; the time in Italy was meant to mark the division, a last hurrah of sorts before I lost my summers to the job. My husband stayed with me for a week before returning to our dog and cats and house. It did not go well. Our Airbnb on Via de' Pepi was swelteringly hot, but open-ing the windows admitted squadrons of black Florentine mosquitoes. We could not get the WiFi to work, and the owner of the flat lived in England. We were halfway to the rental car place when he realized he didn't have the exact address and his cell phone battery died. My husband grew more and more irritable; he'd wanted to re-create *his* Italy for me, and he felt these snafus as personal failures. I was cranky, too. He seemed to want to eat all the time. He simultaneously foisted his friends on me and then awkwardly apologized to them for my reticence. The night before he left, I wept with guilt; we had not made love, I'd held him back from the mythic, romantic Italy he'd known and wanted to give me, and I registered my inhibitions around pleasure as a failure of my own.

I could not have anticipated the turbulence ahead. Later that summer, mere months after Florence, my husband would have major heart surgery, and just weeks after that I would discover his infidelity in the ER, as he suffered the gall bladder attack. I would leave him there to be admitted ("he obviously has people who can take care of him," my sister texted me, sardonically; "get out of that hospital"), drive back in his car to a home and a life irrevocably altered. My husband never came back to our house after that day; life as he'd known it would also collapse. Both of us expelled, you might say, from the garden—though I'm not sure we'd ever thought of paradise in harmonious ways.

Then in 2016, the first summer I wasn't married, still reeling, wondering, *how did it happen?*, the ex of my youth invited me to Italy to teach. Italy: could I do it on my own terms? Except not really *my* terms—some other ex's terms. How to leave the one behind, tending the animals and the house we'd once shared as a married couple, to cavort in Italy with the other? *Italy.* Where my husband and I had thought of retiring, where we'd begun to search for properties online. I'd only ever been to Italy with my husband, the summer after we got married, and then again that summer before we split; Italy was thoroughly bound up with him in my imagination; Italy limned our relationship. It almost didn't exist for me otherwise (the country, I mean, but maybe the marriage too). Going abroad without my husband seemed like a physical impossibility, a violation of space-time. Going with my ex would be a weird pleating of memory.

But we're mature that way, this ex and I, always better friends than lovers anyhow—and he's married now, has twins he adores. He's a poet and a scholar; our intersecting ambitions had been the circulating current of our relationship but also a deadly undertow. When he was leaving me, this poet, he apologized to my soul. We were both so adamantly atheist that we once derailed a dinner party with our godlessly ungenerous insistence that cathedral architecture doesn't prove the divine. And yet the mention of *soul,* whispered with his hand on my chest as if that's actually where it was, did both soothe and undo me, conferring something so serious on his apology, so authentic, that it brought me just to the edge of *belief,* which served only to deepen my grief, even though I'd grown wary (which is a letter away from *weary*) of his guilt and tears. I'd believed we would be together forever, despite the fissures and disputes, just as I'd also believed I'd be married forever, given the intervening years, lessons learned. Both of these men, the poet and the husband, had hurt me badly, as I had hurt them; I value staying connected, the maturity of friendships borne of history and true affection, just as I also sometimes fret that we are all too tentative, bound by our respective anxieties and fear, to make a more definitive break.

I could say no to Italy, then, it's too soon, it'll hurt. Or I could have an adventure, be independent, go on a lark. I could expiate my losses, or dive straight into the belly of it. Bereft of my future, in the company of my past, I could finally "make myself," as the eponymous Sula declares in Toni Morrison's novel, living her "experimental life." Could it be like that, earth "trembl[ing] from her entrails" (9.1000), a great worldly sigh at the moment of reinventing?

Naturally, I went.

IN MILTON'S DAY, young Englishmen of means were just beginning to make routine the post-Oxbridge sojourns in France and Italy that would become known, well into the nineteenth century, as the Grand Tour. These extended trips were far from touristic in any contemporary way, since they were undertaken with specifically educational—often moral and political—intentions, if also to show off a man's prestige both at home and on the Continent. The traveler had a well-defined purpose: he was to soak it all up, the art and music and language, the food and local custom, the national social codes, and thereby augment his sense of knowing *how things are.* The Tour was an eighteen-month study-abroad course in human understanding. Milton embarked in the spring of 1638, when he was twenty-nine. His mother had died the previous spring, and he had spent a now infamously long period of "studious retirement" at his parents' home in west London and later in the hamlet of Horton. He was in Florence from July to September, in Rome by fall and Naples by December. The following spring took him through Lucca, Bologna, Ferrara, Venice, Verona, and Milan, and he was back in England by the summer of 1639, having "met with acceptance above what was looked for."

To imagine that Protestant Milton returned from his travels among Catholic Italians with greater fellow feeling about things like papacy and ecclesiastical hierarchy would be wrong; he had his rigid intolerances, this soon-to-be-radical political theorist. ("I was unwilling to be circumspect in regard to religion," he says in his *Second Defense of the English People* [1092].) Still, he found ready welcome among cadres of writers and artists, scientists and philosophers, whatever differences might have riven their cosmic worldviews. From the exaggerated solitude of studying at home, from the grief of losing a mother, Milton's stay in Italy that year confirmed him in friendship and community. Members of the private learned academies he entered lavished praise upon the young polyglot even before he had left their shores. His linguistic skill, his near-native fluency in Italian, garnered particular admiration, and it's clear from surviving letters and poems that Milton treasured this extended period of intellectual exchange. He'd left home an intense young man who had read just about everything but did not yet know who he was, what to *be*. By the time he got home, he was a poet.

When I try to imagine Milton visiting Galileo, as he did during his two months in Florence, it's like two celestial bodies disengaging from the black backdrop of sky and rearranging themselves beside each other, impossibly far away. An abstraction I can know but not feel, the elderly blind astronomer under house arrest for the heterodoxy of his thinking and the young man searching, wanting so much to matter. A tableau of historical giants taking tea, having coffee, sipping an *aperitivo* fails to take hold in my mind. Did they argue ideas, quote literature, tell a few ribald jokes? There is no record of this encounter beyond Milton's brief mention in *Areopagitica* that he had "visited the famous . . . prisoner to the Inquisition" (and one reference to Galileo's telescope in *Paradise Lost*). Some put this down to the fact that Galileo's science was not revolutionary for Milton, and in any case, the Milton who was himself to become a blind old man under house arrest as a regicide was thirty years in the future.

It's no easier to visualize, really, but I prefer to imagine Milton in the gustatory splendor that is Italy as I've known it, eating the saltless bread of Florence, the risotto of Milan, maybe a Neapolitan flatbread, a *gelato*, a carafe of southern wine, the olives of Sicily. Milton at a long wooden table with the Italian prodigy Carlo Dati—among many others—sopping up the gravy of a roasted wild boar with that dreadful bread, marveling at the unanticipated acceptance: isn't that the very epitome of finding oneself, altered and yet revealed, by travel?

The pleasures of Italy that Milton describes (which may be fewer than the ones he felt) are specifically interpersonal ones: not the beauty of landscape or the delights of cuisine but the reassurance of encounters in the *accademias* that pulled from him his truest convictions. He says frankly in the *Second Defense* that he had "determined within [him]self" not to broach the controversial subject of religion, "but if questioned about [his] faith would hide nothing" (1092). "What I was," he says, "I concealed from no one"—meaning Protestant, of course, but I think also, more simply, *himself,* which is why his account of Italy is dominated by reference to the deep bonds that emerged in spaces of collective learning, in the collision of nations, languages, faiths. Milton felt himself unexpectedly, joyously recognized in Italy, welcomed back by friends he had only just made. Almost a decade after his stay, and in the midst of civil unrest in England, he wrote to Carlo Dati of his sorrow at the news that three letters from Dati had gone astray, and complained that he was daily "teas[ed] and tortur[ed]" by unanticipated visits from people he disliked while the company of those for whom he had real affection was denied by the "cruel distance" between London and his "beloved city" of Florence.

As Milton understood, the delight of feeling nourished in so many aspects of self at once can override quite significant ideological differences. There's pleasure in being invited to take part in a meaningful collective; a more defining joy comes from knowing your presence *constitutes* the collective. Something takes hold—or something lets go—when you understand that success depends on nothing more than your willingness to show up and *be there,* alert and alive to the possibility of it. We can think of this as a kind of holding space, what the British child psychologist D. W. Winnicott referred to as the safe, pleasurable, and intensely creative dynamic of connectedness to another that pertains to good-enough mothering. The companionable silence two people might enjoy, for example, secure in their attachment but thoroughly engaged in separate work—that's holding space, rich in the possibility of independent yet mutual subjectivity. That was Milton's Italy. It is also (obviously but only sometimes) Adam and Eve in Eden, linked in "nuptial League" as they recline, happily eating and conversing, by the bank of a stream, surrounded by gamboling animals, luxuriant in the kind of "dalliance" that "beseems" such a "fair couple" (4.336–40).

And it's my Umbria.

BLAISE PASCAL, that miserable pessimist and French contemporary of Milton, tells us that "[h]uman society is founded on mutual deceit; few friendships would endure if each knew what his friend said of him in his absence" (23). When I deplaned in Rome that 2016 June, boarded a bus with my ex and a dozen or so other jet-lagged travelers, and began a two-hour trek into the hills, I passed some time mentally enumerating all that can go wrong when strangers gather in close quarters. I'm not Raphael, the so-called sociable archangel; I'm Eve, who takes herself off to the garden after a few hours listening to Adam and Raphael discourse about creation, the war in heaven, transubstantiation and the like (*mansplaining* comes unbidden to mind), because "Her husband the Relater she Preferr'd Before the Angel" (8.52). It's not that she's intellectually unsuited to the conversation; it's that Eve, like any self-respecting introvert, prefers a one-on-one. ("Big party, small talk," as a poet I met at a party once declared.) Oh, I expected the worst, I suppose, of name-dropping and cliquishness and worrying about where I'd sit at the communal meals. It doesn't matter how old we are, I think Pascal would agree—we're just kids in a sandbox, tussling over the shovel.

A writer I knew back in graduate school wrote a book of essays about his summers on Martha's Vineyard. If you believe his depiction of events (or, really, my memory—it's been years since I read it), this man enjoyed beach vacations with friends that make *The Big*

Chill look like a nasty British-boarding-school tale of hazing and cruelty. This man had friends who honestly *liked* each other, who slurped up lobster and sweet corn night after night, wiping butter from their chins; drank wine without consequence, inhabited their bodies without embarrassment (thereby slipping out of their colorful shorts and sundresses and into sex, dusted by the grit and salt of the ocean, nightly); thought their poetic thoughts, talked till dawn. That book, which I read in my twenties and quite unfairly hated, felt both nostalgic—evoking memories of childhood before things got messy and affections were easily fractured—and completely alien. Thirty years later I still find myself longing for that kind of group dynamic and simultaneously, veritably, reviling the idea that any good can come of a backyard barbecue. Honestly, whenever I'm invited to one, a part of me hopes I'll get sick.

My husband and I had never figured out how to solve the tension between that kind of introversion and his gregariousness. Over time, it became practically a moral contest. Because we each felt our way in the world to be insulted, we doubled down, we dug in, we fashioned ourselves according to the other's suspicions, we became what we were accused of being. "She's still the shy girl I married," I found out after the fact my husband had emailed a Florentine friend in 2015, maddeningly, as a preemptive excuse for whatever actions of mine he feared he'd not be able to influence after he'd gone home to the States—as if *shy* was all I'd ever be, and the only way he knew to understand, and so excuse, behavior that baffled him. It infuriated me to feel pigeonholed that way, stereotyped—except that it wasn't wrong.

The paradox of entrenching yourself in self-definition is that the role can wear thin. And that's why it's wrong to think that going to another country *doesn't make a difference.* Or maybe it's more accurate to say that we carry with us all the versions of ourselves there are, and when the situation is right, being far away from home with strangers can elicit ones we like a little better. Before my trip to the writers' retreat, I made a promise to myself not to try too hard to recapture an Italian experience I knew had been burnished to a rosy glow by memory, and also not to brace too hard against whatever I feared would go wrong. To just let myself be. I'd gotten so *much* wrong, the previous spring in Florence with my husband, that I didn't want to repeat: the cranky impatience with another person's needs, reining him in as a screen for my own discomfort with letting go. I sensed ahead of time that the circumstances of the conference would not allow me to retreat. So I didn't.

Instead I took a glass of slightly medicinal mint-green liquor someone handed me in a reception room, turned to the woman standing next to me, a librarian from a southern state, and introduced myself. Later I sat down next to someone else from a different southern state, asked her about her job as an editor, and before long we had drunk too much and were laughing like schoolgirls. Let's say the surroundings, the variegated greens of an Italian summer, had prepared us each to receive the heady intensity of workshops, lectures, readings, day trips, and concerts, in a spirit of reciprocity, without pretention or guile. Let's say that, in a multilevel hamlet backed into an Umbrian hill—as if an Escher drawing were the captive audience for another riotous spectacle, one of beech, oak, and laurel trees lined up against fields cleared for farming with white cows grazing in the lower left corner and a full palette below of orange roofing tile and stucco—we got curious again, like children, about the world we inhabit and the people in it. Let's say that, among strangers, we invigorated each other, the teachers and the bankers, the philanthropists and photographers, the ex-high-school football coach and the queer mid-Atlantic poet, the housewives and the MFA students, the lawyers and spoken-word artists and retired physicians.

Let's say that that summer, and every one since, there has been at least one meal, primed by Umbrian Sagrantino and molten cores of smoked mozzarella baked into risotto shaped like a pear, where I end up laughing so hard with the woman sitting next to me (a different one each year) that the men in the room start to get squirrely and jealous. And let's say that, now, I wish I could live always as I have in Umbria. Or no: not as I've lived in Italy. As the person I allow myself to be in Italy. Unencumbered, unafraid. When the ripples of unfamiliarity subside, we discover ourselves anew. The altered perspective helps, but my point is that it's already in us. That it *is* us, this playfully expressive self we can finally feel free enough to release.

*   *   *

WHAT TRAVEL SHARES with religion, as Alain de Botton has said of religion's canny strategy of capitalizing on our need for social belonging, is "joyful immersion in a collective spirit" (37). De Botton writes that religions benefit from the fact that communities solidify in location. A beautiful setting can indeed calm our nerves (to do Burke's philosophy of the sublime an injustice), and so prepare us for encounters with whatever is not-self. The word "kith" is linked etymologically to "couth," which means *mannered* but also *knowing*. To make a friend is to be schooled in the ways of the other.

De Botton further reminds us that "before it was a service, the Mass was a meal" (39). From the moment we sat down to table, unlikely band of pilgrims, taking stock of each other with the *ribollita* and the polenta cake, we were consecrated to each other somehow, invited to shed self-consciousness and fill up with wonder, pleasures of soul inextricable from pleasures of body. (It's Italy, after all; the wine never stops flowing.) This is why Adam and Eve—who of course would never take communion—converse, pray, and dream in the most corporeal of ways, with their fullest embodied selves engaged. Our greatest hilarity would happen at table, and not just because the food was so good. It was there that we learned we could stop rehearsing our worn-out travails (pressed into luggage between the versatile pants and pashminas to be unfolded like delicate rare books we ask our interlocutors to marvel over) and have a different kind of conversation. Let me put it this way: Umbria equalized us as travelers, whether the most important realm we visited was a bike shop in Spoleto where we felt like locals, or the syntactical workings of a poem by Yeats, or the iconography of angels in Italian Renaissance art.

Sharing a meal is just one way we enact the leveling of hierarchy, but it's one Milton elaborates through four books of *Paradise Lost*. Long before they consume bad fruit, Milton's human couple entertain the angel Raphael, who descends like a risen morn to deliver some important news: danger lurks, mind yourselves. Adam has just espied the angel with his six golden wings approaching in a blaze of color "dipped in heaven" (5.283) when he and Eve have a most extraordinary tiff on the subject of "stores." I once made myself the subject of sidelong looks of scholarly consternation at a Milton conference in Yorkshire by contending that the implication of this oddly placed argument is Eve's outright repudiation of all things divine, but that is how I read it: a contest of worldviews occasioned by Adam's command that Eve should "bring forth" what her "stores contain" (5.314) and serve the angel some lunch.

The ostensible gist of their heated exchange is husbandry. Adam imagines that Eve has an extensive larder somewhere from which she will produce a meal fit for an emissary of God, whereas Eve knows that "small store will serve" when, after all, you live in Paradise and "store, / All seasons, ripe for use hangs on the stalk" (5.322–23). In other words, she stores only what's improved by a little "firmness" (324) and drying out; otherwise, she fairly smirks, who needs a pantry in the garden of Eden?

But there's much more at stake in these twenty lines. (There has to be a point, structurally speaking, of delaying the arrival of an angel.) For one thing, angels make Adam nervous in a fanboy/First-of-Men kind of way—that middle position he occupies as student of divine beings and teacher of Eve fills him with pedagogical anxiety—to say nothing of the admission he will make to Raphael as the afternoon deepens that he's pretty sure Eve already knows everything on her own. Thence his operatic command to "bring forth and pour / Abundance" (314–15), to "bestow" (317) upon their "givers their own gifts," as if to say that appreciation is always an *economic* rather than interpersonal transaction and when you suspect yourself of terrible *ontological* insufficiency, all you can do is turn apparent beneficence back on itself, masking what you're afraid you can't afford. Eve, in response to such torturous reasoning about a strange kind of Edenic tax, points out that sycophantic appeasement is irrelevant to her intimate understanding of the natural world. It's nothing to her to select the "juiciest" (327) and choicest gourds and plants because for Eve the garden is the place she is most *herself,* to impose a modern vernacular—free from the kind of hierarchal logics by which Adam struggles to locate his proper place. "Beholding" what they have to offer, Eve says, Raphael "shall confess that here on earth," they serve up better than any old celestial ambrosia (329).

I love to teach this scene because it condenses so many of the poem's philosophical investments. When Eve goes on to "temper" (5.347) kernels to creams, she isn't just *juicing;* when she decides what "choice to choose" (333) in a not "inelegant" (335) mixture, she isn't being finicky. She's enacting the principle that *truth* has multiple shapes, that unity is found not in sameness but in plurality, that eating abundantly but well is different from the mindless consumption of gluttony (an insult that Milton reserves for Sin, Death, and corrupt friars). To temper is to blend—and, with connotations of tempering metal, to strengthen by bringing unlikes together. Eve will be just as "unsparing" (344) as Adam hoped to be "large" (317) with this meal. But where Adam's notion of "stores" is an undifferentiated sweep complicated by his sense of being *burdened* rather than enlivened by earthly tasks and earthly multiplicity, Eve makes cooking a matter of selection that can only be done well when you know—really know—everything in its individual nature. This is cooking as ethical dialectic, to be artful in the preservation, and the synthesis, of distinction. Eve is a locavore, and she's not afraid of difference.

Two things have always mattered to me in this culinary scenario: one, dinner parties can surface our most fiercely held beliefs, and two, coupled people will inevitably argue about that. I could not have anticipated that a ten-day conference in Umbria, summer camp for grown-ups, Vegas for arty nerds, would end up being the very crucible in which Eve tempers her fruits, creating me anew.

UMBRIA MEANS SHADE, as in umbrella, burnt umber, or taking umbrage (which should etymologically connote refuge but instead is resentment, as in the murky darkness of petty self-righteousness). The ancient people called Umbri inhabited the shadows of this centermost region of the boot, Italy's "green heart," contoured by the hills and dense forests. Much later Francis of Assisi, patron saint of animals and ecology, lived in a grotto of rock above Spoleto, smaller than a linen closet, for more than a year.

I learned that as a young man, Francis developed a spiritual practice that alternated between periods of intense solitude and communal devotion, each nourishing (maybe stoking the need for) the other. One year, a few months before the Italy conference, I'd been to a meditation retreat, a form of solitude-in-company that a woman in Italy named Joan (who had a reverence for Francis that was unperformed) likened to Francis in hermitage. I was thinking more of Eve wanting to garden alone as the counterpoint to her enjoyment of conversation with Adam. Conversation, as Milton so adamantly declared in his defense of divorce, is both the cornerstone of good marriage and a fully embodied act—at its best, intellectual and sensory at once and thus a very charged affair, erotic and psychically intense. Some of us (I suspect Francis was one) don't transition easily from the recuperations of being alone to that sort of contact. Then again, solitude can be crushing.

It was challenging, that first summer at the conference, to keep the parts of my life and self protectively separated without dissociating. Everything seemed tinged with regret about the future I wasn't anymore living my way into, from the medieval hamlet my husband would have loved to have a hand in restoring to the very notion of an artists' retreat, such as the one he'd tried to establish years ago in the South of France. I would hole up in my sun-filled flat (or awaken at 3:00 a.m.) and nurse the lonesomeness, which was complicated by layers of loss: I was there, after all, with another man I'd once anticipated spending my life with. But on my very first evening in Umbria, that ex knocked on my door to call me forth, into the gathering of happy travelers at the *enoteca*, drinking Aperol spritzes and chilled Orvieto. I'd been dozing on the couch, bleary with jetlag and sadness, and then I crossed a literal threshold into an atmosphere guileless and gorgeous with sunset, with people who didn't know, and couldn't feel, any of my painful history. Anyway, we all had our stories—the "handpicked days [of] memory," in Natasha Trethewey's words, "preserved" in "our minds' dark pantry"—which we would offer to each other or not, over the days and nights, according to our whims.

In the misted coolness of St. Francis's sacred woods, holy oaks mimic the forms of animals. Their trunks swirl into conversations with themselves, cast their shapes on carpets of leaves so thick that footfalls are instantly absorbed and everyone around you seems to undulate, as if under water. It would be terrifying, I think, at night. To get to the tiny cave Francis lived in, you descend a steep, rocky incline, make a sharp left. You'd have to know the woods intimately, you'd have to trust the woods, utterly, to find that dark hole, to find home in that darkness, before the ropes and markers that over the centuries have made it a shrine. You'd have to believe, as Francis did, that you could emerge back into the sunlight, find your way back up through the shrubbery and stones, reach out to your brothers, sit down again to a meal.

WHAT DOES A WOMAN look like, walking in the rain across Florence, carrying a standing fan? Let me flash back again, to that first spring in 2015, before it all changed.

My husband used to say that he was never in such good shape as the two years he lived in Florence, because Italians approach meals as slow, deliberate affairs, and you end up learning how to gauge your hunger, how to care for the longings but also to respect the limits of the body. Maybe, if that's the kind of compassionate self-care you're capable of. The afternoon I carried a borrowed fan from my apartment on Via de' Pepi across town to Santino's for a lunch of bean soup and fried *caciocavallo* (a type of cheese made in the shape of saddle bags), it was mid-May and drizzling. My husband had gone back to the States and left me in the care of his gaggle of local friends, including Santino, who taught English in high school by day and sang Broadway songs to tourists from Denmark and Japan around town at night. His rendition of *Phantom* was, if he did say so himself, legendary.

I was feeling ready to go home. The strain of maneuvering in a language I'm not good at and a solitude I'd hoped would be more liberating and courageous had wormed its way into my sense of myself. Santino also seemed tired that day, I remember. The meal felt forced (he offered day-old desserts from his gig at a hotel the night before), and I left as soon as it was polite to do so, weaving my way home through hordes of tourists. I was not at all attracted to Santino, an Italian man who had me over for a lunch of stale bread and wine in his flat overlooking the Arno, in the absence of my husband, and I was both relieved and disappointed about that. I did not yet know that my husband was himself not exactly honoring the vows of our marriage.

Accepting an invitation to lunch with my husband's friend, in his absence, was supposed to be a victory of sorts, proof that I wasn't socially phobic. The truth is that for all my storied love of solitude, I was not having a grand time on my own; I spent hours in the rented flat reading Harry Potter in Italian and trying to figure out how to order in Italian, because I fixated on the idea that the singular act of asking another person for food in a language not my own exemplified a self-confidence I craved—to be embodied, intimate, and imperfect, all at once.

Toward the start of that luncheon in *Paradise Lost*, Raphael tells Adam and Eve that "whatever was created, needs / To be sustained and fed"—even angels (5.414–15). Call it ambrosia, but angels still need to eat, for food is vital to the "concoction" of intellect, imagination, self. The epic abounds with references to digestion, because eating represents the very foundation of how we become who we are. It isn't just physical sustenance. Nor is the process of taking in, breaking down, converting, and absorbing just a metaphor for other kinds of interaction between self and world; it is literal. For "knowledge is as food," as Raphael also says (7.126), and bodies and minds exist only in tandem with each other. Milton had a particular horror of gluttony, because the idea of swallowing *anything* whole, without thoughtfully chewing it up first, incorporating it into awareness, is rash, impetuous, and uncritical. Digestion (as my student had rightly insisted) was one of his most powerful symbols for activating the very fullest of ourselves through everything that can be gleaned from beyond our own perimeters: books, conversation, experience.

There's a reason this lesson happens at mealtime. Only when we lean all in, bodyminds in a state of heightened readiness for what's about to breach our thresholds, do we grow.

ON ONE OF OUR last nights in Italy, on the fourth summer of the conference, my ex and I had a confab about the past—about mistakes we'd made and regrets we had, traumas whose governing power over our actions we'd only just realized the strength of. We needed just a few words to heal: *I'm sorry, I was broken, I'll always love you, we were so young.* It felt refreshingly *realistic* somehow. Clarifying. As if we hadn't grasped until that moment, seventeen years after we split, exactly what had happened between us.

Then he said, "What's going on in your marriage?"

It wasn't the first time he'd asked, and I felt a shiver of embarrassment that what I was about to say wouldn't sound all that new. "We . . . have our thing," I said, vaguely, hearing the twinge of defensiveness. I said, "we're still married, for now." I said we had no intention of trying again. I explained about the dog and the house my husband had practically rebuilt in our years together and the ease and comfort of asking him for help when I needed it. I mentioned health issues and health insurance and the insignificant costs to me, all things considered, of not having to pay spousal support to a self-employed ex-husband. I admitted that guilt is likely a factor in all of this. I understand that my husband wants to do what he can for me, that what he can do is often more practical than emotional, and that such an arrangement works for both of us, that it's both redemptive and exculpatory. The anguish of separation, so shocking and abrupt, had been unbearable; holding onto each other in this liminal way is reassuring.

What I wanted to say to my ex was, what happened had felt like a violent upending—like everything was irrevocably lost. And yet, after a few years, I realized the ship had righted itself. I'd carried on, despite my terror of the unknown. We'd settled into a routine that maximized what was always best in our relationship—casual laughter about the antics of the dog, TV we'd watch together and projects devised for the yard, cocktails only he and I knew the names of and conversations about politics, Buddhism, family, and work. Then he'd drive off again, leaving a welcome quiet behind. Aren't there plenty of married couples who'd actually prefer to live apart?

I thought the man sitting next to me in Italy would grasp my meaning. After all, we too once represented the future to each other. But we were so young; I was twenty-five when we met. It's right that we grew up, into other versions of ourselves, into other loves and new lives we struggle at, just like the old ones. I've always been a little proud to know that we've held on to those naïve kids, who we were to each other when life crushed us, sometimes, with its enormity— even as we uncover who we are to each other now, in our fifties, when friendships seem harder to cultivate and so worthy of our care.

"I want that love in my life," I said, "as complicated as it is."

My ex shifted a little in his chair, and I worried he was about to protest to me that I needed to proceed to divorce. It isn't healthy, or something along those lines, to stay in limbo.

Instead he said, "I agree with you," just like that.

I LIKE TO THINK this conversation could only have happened in Italy, where the phases of our lives concertina and we can call upon our mutual past to offer solace for the woes of our respective presents. Or maybe it just makes sense in Italy, where I feel so acutely that loss of a certain kind of life for another I can't foresee. Well, certainty about the arc of life is always an illusion, as Milton also understood; his own time in Italy was cut short by the death of his beloved friend Charles Diodati back home, as well as by impending civil war. Did Milton know, as I learn from reading de Botton, that "spirits from the coast- line south of Naples . . . were thought to be particularly well suited to the abatement of melancholy" (268)? How did *I* not know until now that "[u]nhappily married women went to Umbria to visit the shrine of St Rita of Cascia, patron saint of marital problems" (271)? When I look up Saint Rita, I discover that there's a National Shrine to her in Philadelphia, my hometown, adjacent to the hometown of my ex. Can I admire that convergence, without believing in Rita as a saint? De Botton (who had the inspired idea of writing a whole book while/ about sitting in an airport) says that travel can "salve the wounded parts of us" (272), even if we're not on spiritual pilgrimage. Can an atheist travel to heal, not just to be entertained or to escape? Milton did not abandon his eclectic, protesting beliefs during his sojourn in Catholic Italy. He just made room for other pleasures and pursuits. Got out of the way, so to speak, of the self he was becoming.

Umbria, then: my garden, my revelation. I haven't wanted to re- hearse the travel-transcendence paradigm, the whole Tuscan sun, eat-pray-whatever cliché of a heartbroken woman who discovers her- self in the redemptive balm of dislocation, losing weight on a diet of sumptuous local fare, stumbling her way toward fast friendships in a language she doesn't speak, getting geographically lost in tiny villages to find her spiritual way. But alright, meeting the man of your dreams aside, some experiences do distill down to pure joy. For a woman so suspicious of happiness that the very word smacks my ears like the sound of a plastic kazoo, Umbria is another of my versions of the ecstasy of faith.

As for these men of the past, I can't quite quit them. Or maybe it's better just to keep posing the question: do I need to? We think of our stories as linear, and we crave them to help ourselves make sense, for solace and closure and freedom from guilt. But they're circular, too, looping and recursive, like those tiny pawprints in the snow of the dog Jack, not at all lost but exploring, delighting in it—Jack on his own Grand Tour—and only eventually, when he got tired, making his way home, a home that had a new cat in it, instead of a man. Milton returned from Italy revivified and mature, ready to take on a career of philosophical intensity, that would be shaped by war, complicated by marriage, ultimately defined by steadfast conviction and a headlong tilt into verse. Most lives are humbler than that, of course, tangled up in ordinary disappointments, only occasional joys. Most of us are losing our bearings, dismantling ourselves, searching, *aching*, you might say, for what to believe, and how to know it. The transcendent sense of belonging I've felt at the conference in Umbria evaporates, inexorably, once I'm home again, restored to the usual routines of a life. That's just what travel is like. But I can carry this consolation secure within me, as Eve will say at the end of her tale: that I once sat down to a meal in Umbria, surrounded by acceptance and laughter, and there I was.

7

WILD WORK

IN THE MOMENTS just after she has eaten a forbidden apple, the Eve of *Paradise Lost* contemplates what will happen if the death that was threatened as punishment actually—or eventually—"ensue[s]." "Then I shall be no more," she thinks, "And *Adam* wedded to another *Eve*, / Shall live with her enjoying, I extinct." This image of another woman is too much to stand, and moments later she approaches Adam with her secret and her fruit, "resolve[d]" to endure "with him all deaths" (9.827–32). Adam in turn also forms a "resolution . . . to Die," so painful is the thought of life without the "sweet Converse and Love" of one "so dearly joyn'd" to him, even if he could expect God to "create another Eve" (9.907–11).

The fact that both immediately assume "another Eve" is unsurprising—the future of humanity as Milton understood it depends on that kind of coupling—but the triangulations they imagine are not quite the same. Confronted with the possibility of losing Eve, Adam envisions carrying on with a second wife in a way that seems fraught with fear of *loneliness*, a recurrence of the solitariness and dis-ease that characterized his earliest moments in the garden. For Eve, it is *replacement* that dominates the fantasy, fear that Adam will not mourn her loss because his attention will be captivated elsewhere. It's the thought of Eve's demise that occasions this difference, of course, in those few suspended moments before Adam too decides to eat, and so also to die. And it's a short path from this moment of epic tension—*the* instant in which the fate of human history will be sealed—to me awake in the wee hours of a night, wondering what would happen if I stormed a certain hair salon in a neighboring town and demanded the owner keep her damned cheating hands off my husband.

I Facebook-stalked them both for a while, the way you do, as if catching them at it after the fact would validate something, register somehow. *What would she do?* I asked him, of the hair-salon-sortie. *Would she feel regret?* No, he said; she'd be angry. (We imagine that others are thinking about us, but honestly, they rarely are). What would it matter anyway? I couldn't make myself drive into that town. The last time we were there together, when the lawyer finalized our separation agreement and my husband was barely recovered from having his gall bladder out, I wept helplessly into the steering wheel of my car while he crouched in the open driver's side door, sweating and holding my hand.

From a hospital bed he had told me he was in love with us both. I'd forgotten that until just the other day, reading back through years of texts with my sister, to a message I'd sent her on the fourth day after I discovered it all. He loved his other Eve, he'd said, but he wanted his life with me.

I extinct.

MILTON FIERCELY BELIEVED that choice is inherent in the human condition of free will. "Reason also is choice," says God in *Paradise Lost* (3.108), sounding like his author, who believed angels and humans alike to be "authors to themselves in all" (122). *Areopagitica,* Milton's spirited argument against the licensing of books, defends a kind of greedy reading as the necessary foundation of an active and engaged citizenry: only by having the freedom to encounter both "good" and "bad" ideas through books do we cultivate the intellectual discernment that will foster our search for truth, defined as a multitude of differing parts. Liberty of conscience is synonymous with being able to make our own decisions, the author declares; censorship infantilizes us, and human rationality, in its best incarnation, guarantees critical thinking. Milton was no fan of what he calls "glutton friars," and reserved his worst condemnations for church officials who hoard knowledge by suppressing the publication of books and who presume to impose doctrine on naïve and trusting flocks. He writes,

"I cannot praise a fugitive and cloistered virtue, unexercised and un-breathed, that never sallies out and sees her adversary," impatient with the idea that a church presumes to protect its members by de-priving them of opportunity to actively and actually test themselves in challenging circumstances (939). "Wherefore did he create passions within us, pleasures round about us?" he asks. (Indeed.) "Reason is but choosing" (944). To be deprived of the capacity to choose is to be "captivate[d] under a perpetual childhood of prescription" (938).

Think about it: we make hundreds of choices every day. Most of them are innocuous—these shoes, that shortcut to work, a glass of rosé or a bottle of beer. Some are more like the pendant world Mil-ton imagined hanging in the cosmos, with everything in the balance, all manner of boisterous life and possible mayhem concealed within, ready to burst forth. We tend to think of those bigger decisions we make in a life—jobs, purchases, relationships, kids—as requiring a lot of us: our considered attention, consultation with our besties, a pros-and-cons list, and plenty of time. But isn't it really smaller than that, a whole series of moves we barely notice that got us from *there* to *here?* All the fretting and stewing we do, *should I/shouldn't I,* can it ever fully account for unconscious longings and fears?

And another thing. All this focus on the effects of single choices—that first bite of the apple, that night he let her climb . . . no, that night *he kissed her back*—doesn't that obsession with singularity ignore everything that came before? Where am *I* in the idea that our lives di-vided irrevocably only on that night, in that minute, in those few *sec-onds* when she leaned forward and he opened his mouth, let her place her tongue on his, lifted her shirt and put his hand on her breast? Did our marriage really fail *on a dime,* as I've written and believed, in the instant I found their texts? What I mean is, even as I blamed him for certain choices he'd made, even as I felt I'd gone with him to the hos-pital as one sort of woman and come home again, four hours later, as entirely another, I had trouble getting angry. I had some work to do, I felt, to understand what had brought us there, over time and as a couple, to that terrible brink.

One night in Eden, Eve has a strange dream in which a being "shaped and winged like one of those from heaven" (5.55) tempts her to eat from the forbidden tree and then flies her up to the sky to behold all of earth below. In the morning she recounts the dream to Adam, and he, though troubled by these "uncouth" (98) imaginings, is quick to reassure his wife that just because we dream a desire doesn't mean we'll act on it: "what in sleep thou didst abhor to dream, / Waking thou never wilt consent to do" (120–21). Reason may be "chief" among our faculties, he tells her (102), but at night, with reason relaxed, "fancy" wakes up and starts its "wild work" (112) of mixing up memories and thoughts until we can no longer properly identify their shapes. Evil will "come and go," he tells her, uninvited, into our hearts and minds, but it leaves "no spot or blame behind" (118–19).

The point is that Milton's Eve is no innately sinful temptress; she's blameless till she does that one deed forbidden to her. In fact, nothing we might think of as having suspiciously sinful potential, like sex or eating, is rendered as such in *Paradise Lost* (this is why angels cavort with their boneless bodies after treating each other to ambrosia). It's all about intentionality—the spirit we bring to the thing.

But this is tricky territory, and I think Milton knew it. *I didn't mean to hurt you!* Has such an excuse ever been enough? *It didn't mean anything!* Doesn't everything mean *something?*

MILTON WAS EVENTUALLY reconciled to Mary Powell, his first wife, after living apart for three years. Mary would die in childbirth. Milton's second wife, Kathryn Woodcock, also died from complications of childbirth. Only Elizabeth Mynshull, whom he married in 1662, would survive him (they were thirty-one years apart). She is known from an inscription in a stone set in her uncle Thomas's house as Milton's "3rd and Best wife." But many scholars consider Kathryn to have been the favorite, based at least in part on the only extant poem addressed to one of Milton's spouses, so-called sonnet 19, "On His Late Wife," in which the speaker's "late espoused saint" appears to him in a dream.

I've never spent enough time in class with this record of a failed wish-fulfillment, which owes its weirdness to Milton's characteristically brilliant syntax. There's a woman in white, her face "veiled" (Milton was blind when he married Kathryn), her "person" shining with love and goodness. She's the epitome of purity (even the name

Kathryn has been connected to the Greek *katharos*, meaning pure), and—or maybe, *therefore*—the speaker wakes up before they can "embrace." No sullying sexuality in this dream! It's the order of actions that intrigues me. In the last line, "I waked, she fled, and day brought back my night." Inevitable disappointment, we may think; how often have any of us awakened still alone (or still unhappy), tangled in sweaty sheets with a dog breathing softly (or a man snoring loudly), in the dark? But Milton's line does something curious in making the woman flee *after* the man has awakened, as if *he's* the one to reject her touch. It was *she* who had "inclined" to embrace him, after all. Does he fear what he thinks he wants? And maybe, even worse, does he suspect she never wanted him in the first place? He saves himself from such implications by staging it all through the mechanics of sleep. He couldn't help it, the poem says. His body woke him up. We can't fault anyone, either the apotheosis of "sweetness" or the insecure man, for the crisis of their disappointed intimacy.

It was Milton who coined the words *debauchery, besottedly, sensuous, jubilant, irresponsible, enjoyable,* and *love-lorn.* The poet did understand pleasure, the need for it, the joys of it, the *unaccountable* force of it (another of his coinages). I've read that while he and Mary were apart, he tried to convince one Miss Davis that he would remain a marriageable man even if he divorced his wife. His reputation as an advocate of temperance and chastity has obscured something else of the man he was, eager for passionate attunement. He also so privileged humans' ability to reason their way through the thickets of *self-delusion* that I wonder if he didn't falsely minimize the power of "fancy," the way it distracts and preoccupies us, ruining concentration, making all kinds of wrongdoing seem legitimate, viable, even righteous. *Vindicated:* that's the word my husband used to describe what he felt after that first threshold-crossing kiss, righteous in having a taste of what he thought he was due, a little happiness in the midst of months of struggle. It's also how God seems to feel, telling the Son that all creatures, even "faithless" humans, are "made just and right, / Sufficient to have stood, though free to fall" (3.96, 98–99)—unconscious, it would seem, of his own powerful need for the "proof" (103) and "pleasure" (107) of love given "freely," uncoerced (102). It's how Satan feels, down in the "mournful gloom" (1.244), when he delivers that most famous line, "Better to reign in hell, than serve in heaven" (263). So too did I think I was choosing rightly in asking a man to marry me, choosing against type, not being "led," finally, "by libido," as I and some of my maturing women friends liked to say of ourselves, choosing for *character* instead. It's empowering to conduct ourselves this way, according to the endowment of choice. To believe we're in control.

Nine months after we split up, I dreamt that my husband was living in my childhood bedroom. My own apartment was across the hall, in my sister's old room. I snuck into his place one day when he was away from this amalgam of memory and loss, laid down on his bed to try to get the scent of him. *What are we doing?*, I thought in the dream. *We should just get back together.*

THE OPPOSITE OF choice is compulsion. Plenty of critical ink has been spilled on the scene in which Eve describes meeting Adam for apparently grinding our noses in male dominion. She'd just been exchanging glances with a face in a pool, she tells him (she didn't yet know it was herself), when she was pulled away from that pleasurable encounter by an authoritarian voice who commands her to follow, promising to take her to one she'll "enjoy / inseparably thine" (4.472–73). "What could I do," she asks Adam in this present moment, "But follow straight, invisibly thus led?" (475–76). Such words connote helplessness, not want. And what's worse, when she saw him, Eve continues, though he was "fair indeed and tall," she found Adam "*less* fair, / *Less* winning soft, *less* amiably mild," than that other face (477–79)—I'm adding the emphasis—and "back [she] turned" (480). It's not explicitly told what ultimately unites them. He claimed her as his "other half," she reminds him (488). He "seized" her hand (489).

We hear a different version of the scene much later in the poem, when Adam implies to Raphael that Eve "turned" (8.507) *so that* she would be followed: she would "not unsought be won," he says, but rather "would be wooed" (503). It's a dance of honor, in this account, but also, given what we already know from Eve herself, an embarrassing miscalculation. Students sometimes snigger with derision at poor Adam, puffing himself up before the angel like an outmoded Renaissance courtier and misinterpreting entirely his wife's emotional self. I'd say it's both comical and terribly sad, if you imagine them both having turned, expectantly and with love, toward the world—she to the one she was just discovering, he to the one he'd been promised— and missing each other this way. They've been formed as paradigms, she as "Mother of human race" (4.475) and he as "patriarch of mankind" (9.376), constructs that inhibit the kind of energetic, honest conversation Milton everywhere styles as intersubjective knowing, and it takes nothing less than the furious rending of trespass to guide them back to each other in less delimiting guises.

I realize in explaining how I interpret these scenes that that's what I thought my own rupture would produce: hard-won but lyrically ecstatic reconciliation. Because I've read *Paradise Lost*, framed it this way for myself, so many times. It's pure coincidence, of course, that I too turned away at first from my husband (after a handful of dates), unsure of how I felt or what I wanted, and that we had very different explanations for the two-month hiatus we took (that I forced) before I turned toward him again. "That time you dumped me," he used to say, usually in front of other people, and I would want to cry out in defense of my right to choose for myself: I didn't *dump* you, we weren't a couple, and *who* proposed to *whom* in the end? We carried that clash of feeling—the shame, resentment, and indignation, the confusion that having chosen, that *being* chosen, somehow wasn't enough—well into and to other side of marriage.

Just about everything that happens in *Paradise Lost* might be understood as dramatizing the answer to Eve's question, "What could I do?" We can always choose to resist, or pause and question, or be brave and investigate. If it's right for Eve to follow one voice, why would it be intrinsically wrong, later on, to follow a talking snake—and if one following is a sin, why isn't the other? Setting up such radical equivalences is how the epic reminds us that even if we're constantly being *led* in this life—by interest, desire, obligation, force—we never lose our capacity to get thoughtful about it. All manner of figures in the poem presume to inform Eve about who she is and how she ought to think about herself. It's up to her, with all her sensory and intellectual resources, to decide for herself. Just because *voices* might articulate patriarchal hierarchy doesn't mean the poem endorses them.

Of course, even as I contemplate the poem's invitation to work our way out of coercive narration, I risk boxing myself in again. I'm not *actually* patterning my marriage on Milton's Adam and Eve (honestly!). But Milton has infiltrated, surely, as a set of possibilities I've devoted myself to in the absence of religious faith. I *wish* I could live in the fullness of Miltonic choice, even if the reality of life is so much more complicated, its variables so much harder to predict, than a single nefarious angel hovering at the periphery of your vision. Milton knew that too, of course, elsewhere figuring experience as the avalanche of indistinguishable seeds that Psyche must sort through, which is how we arrive at truth. I've admired, for so long, the wife's fierce independence, and how the husband tries after all his obtuse misapprehension of her motives to generate "matrimonial love" (9.319). How they manage, according to their temperaments, to skirt doctrinal pressure. It's not literal, this mapping of myself along the travails and triumphs of a poetic human pair; it's connected to how the author's ideas activate a desirous, intellectual part of myself.

I wish real life could feel the way I do when I'm inside of that poetry, if that makes any kind of sense. In the pleasure of writing about a couple who do what they must to become understood. There may be nothing more erotic, I sometimes think, *sublimating*, or just geeking out entirely, than how it feels to write about *Paradise Lost*.

So WHAT HAS CHOICE to do with happenstance? With all that aimless but somehow intentional wandering that happens in the chaotic universe of this epic poem? How do I square the very things I love about Milton's depiction of nature—that it's process- rather than goal-oriented, that differences proliferate rather than being contained, that "rapture" can be defined as a river wending its way (7.299), all that dog-in-the-snowy-woods self-care—with a sense that we're also in charge of choosing for ourselves? How self-authored are we really, if we believe in the undertow of the unconscious?

In Genesis 3, it takes a mere six verses, some dozen lines of text, for the serpent to work his wiles and Adam and Eve to eat from the forbidden tree. In Milton's book, nearly two hundred lines of poetry are devoted just to an argument between the human pair that offers context for why it is that Eve eats first. It's another four hundred lines before she actually bites the apple. The expansion—and the delay—are significant, not so much because they heighten suspense (we know what's coming), but because we get to witness all the disputation that happens before any singular act. This is it, after all, *the* choice that's at the heart of "all our woe" (1.3), and the epic thoroughly dramatizes how smart, rational, inherently good beings come to make a particularly bad decision.

Because you don't just grab it and eat it, that forbidden fruit, *rashly*, even if it seems that way; it's been building up in you over lines and stanzas and whole epic books. And maybe you're a faulty empiricist, misreading the evidence of your environment, thinking that something makes sense when it ought to set off alarm bells. (And really, isn't a talking snake, with "his turret crest, and sleek enameled neck, / Fawning, and lick[ing] the ground" you walk on, absolutely the best metaphor for every bad date you've ever been on? [9.525–26].) Or an overzealous empiricist, trusting your gut more than the teachings you ought to, and do, believe in. Maybe the constant flux of boundaries in the relationship has gotten so taxing, with his nervousness (if also love) that makes him want to keep you by his side. (Maybe he thinks you *came* from his side, a "subducting" he can't seem to get over [8.536]; literalist that he is, on your second or third date you joked that you wanted him to plan your dates forever, and he thought you really meant it, *forever,* so he was devastated when you disappeared.) You just want to garden by yourself for a while, test your strength, because "Eden were no Eden" if you live in it constantly in fear of threat (9.341). And "what is faith, love, virtue unassayed / Alone" (335)?

No such thing as cloistered virtue, that's the point; you have to be tested. You're "yet sinless" (659) for a good long time, by the way, everyone should know this, even when your "eager appetite" awakens—it's "noon," for goodness sake; you're hungry—at the foot of that tree no one can stop talking about (739–40). Yet *still* you pause to muse over the matter (744). Even the *serpent* takes a breath, struck "stupidly good" by your innocence, utterly "disarmed / Of guile, of hate, of envy, of revenge" (465–66). That's mindfulness in a nutshell. That fraction of an instant between all the roiled-up emotion, the talking-yourself-into-it, and actually doing it, whatever "it" is. Deep breath before you've plunged forward, "plucked" and "ate" (781).

But there it is. You *reasoned* your way into it. Maybe you did have the best intentions. Maybe you honestly didn't know how bad it was going to get. *You* is the woman, who ate first, is me, restless for independence; is him, the husband, who chose his other Eve; all of us entangled in these choices we want to feel fully in charge of.

It's comforting to think so, of course, that we're in charge that way, from those mountains upheaving themselves into the sky to "whatever creeps the ground" (7.475). And we are, in the sense of inhabiting a world without predestination, or being able to own up to our errors. "God left free the will," Adam says (9.351). But will can be "misinformed" (355). Call that snake a projection of all we can never be fully guarded against, no matter how closely we stick together, or how resilient we feel in ourselves—call that fruit a representation of our longings, our mendacity, our basically conflicted natures. The dilemma isn't whether we'll want that "thing not undesirable" (exquisite Miltonic double negative) (9.824). Because we will. We do.

The agonizing question wasn't why he started it, but why he didn't stop.

MAYBE THE OPPOSITE of choice is inertia. The affair wasn't a fling; it lasted more than two years. He told me he had been in the process of organizing himself to end it when his heart gave out. Maybe the stress was too much, to put a causal spin on things. Maybe the center could not hold.

I have this suspicion that everyone wants to know why I'm not divorced. What that really means is, I want to know why I'm not divorced. After some amount of time, a year of couples' therapy, *are you–aren't you* inquiries (and a few times, maddeningly, royal-"do we know yet . . .?" to which I finally answered, *who's we?* I mean, seriously!), and various recalibrations of the frame of it—Married-Living-Apart is a trend, though I bet they mostly don't have legal separation agreements gathering dust in a closet upstairs, those independent coupled souls, the details of its financial terms largely forgotten or ignored—anyway, I got tired of "doing" this marriage-that-wasn't. I wanted a year or more where *he* was not the thing that structured my thinking. I would take a break, work on friendships, strengthen myself, learn to be content in my solitariness. Me, the dog, the cat, in the house I kept not being able to stop asking him to do things to. (It's a mouthful on purpose.)

In that state of aggravation about the limbo we were in, I called the office of the mediator who'd drawn up our agreement. There was something I didn't understand about where it was being stored, in a drawer at the lawyer's instead of filed with a judge, and I thought that moving it from one place to the other would kick in some legal meaningfulness with which I could signal to the husband that I meant *business*. Except the woman on the phone told me location didn't matter, it was legal the minute we'd all signed the thing however many months before. There've been plenty of moments like this in the last six years, where I get serious and start divvying up the belongings, disentangling the car insurance, getting him to *finally* pay a guy to remove the truck bed that was disintegrating in the side yard, whole hunks of rusted metal settling into the earth. Moments of self-definition and empowerment, of setting limits.

I know that some of my friends assume I'm divorced, and when they find out I'm not, wonder if it's because I want to reconcile with my husband. Most of them stopped interrogating the status of my marriage when we quit couples' therapy and it was obvious my husband wasn't moving back in. No one ever came right out and told me to kick him to the curb, but I knew that some of them wished it for me, that dramatic assertion of independence, the galvanizing momentum of anger. Others had urged me to give him—give *us*—another chance. Deep, mature love is rare, after all. The vows should mean something; working on love when it seems frailest and most frayed is precisely how we honor it.

These have always seemed the two, and only, options: reconciliation or divorce.

But extended separation? That kind of suspension doesn't make sense. It emanates a whiff of something untoward. Ambivalence. A cowardly indecision. Or worse: my own embarrassingly low self-esteem. An unfeminist inability to stick up for myself. Whenever people praise me for being "compassionate" toward a husband whose infidelity I discovered when he was literally lying in a hospital bed, whose material circumstances have always been more precarious than mine, I suspect what they really mean is "weak." Even our therapist got impatient with us after about six months, when we were no nearer to taking definitive action than the first afternoon we'd sat down in her office, my husband cracking dull, self-protective jokes and me staring at her ocean-colored toenails peeking through her sandals, feeling hopeless and mute.

So, not divorced, because like I said, breathless panic, a look that came over his face when I said *I thought you knew that's where this was headed* and the feeling I got—get—thoracic constriction, when I think about calling (say) a "handyman" instead of *him* when the closet door comes off its hinges. I'm happier by myself, I'll say it again (and maybe it'll truly sink in, in the retelling) but astonished nonetheless at the failure of it, the murky *this-ness* of how it happens that you end up somewhere instead of arriving at your destination. I could offer the practical justification that staying married is financially beneficial to us both, at least for now. A few friends have worried that not divorcing would hold me back from new romance. Until recently, I had no interest in that sort of exploration, and recently, when I did, I felt no obligation to a marriage-that-isn't. But what *is* it, exactly? I don't *feel* "married." What's wrong with holding on to an affection that means you have someone to call when a tree comes down on your roof?

But this is far from a matter of efficiency. It's about what happens when the shadows of an afternoon creep into your bones like a damp chill, and you feel like the last living soul on earth. Isn't the important thing to keep mattering to each other, if we're able to redefine a love? In fact to redefine rather than sacrifice, to carry on contouring ourselves within its fortifying strengths? In the first agonizing weeks of being separated, I would sometimes think, *so this is what it feels like.* ("I unbuckled myself from a man / and stood," says the speaker of "Tandem," by Lyrae Van Clief-Stefanon, "on my own shaking legs.") We're inured to the ubiquity of marriages ending over affairs. It's practically glamorous, or at least, narratively *interesting.* (Think of Showtime's *The Affair,* where just about every revelation of infidelity seems to land the offended party in someone else's bed rather than a lawyer's office.) The casual statistic that half of all marriages end in divorce completely obscures how wrenching it actually is. When I worry the most about my inability to take some self-determining action, I immediately want to defend my right to ward off further sorrow.

THE FIRST TIME I went to my not-husband's house, at least three years after we split, and I saw the space he'd created for himself, I felt a jolt of envy, coming face-to-face with how his life had carried on in my absence, just as mine had in his. Then I felt glad. It was so quintessentially *him*, the paint colors I'd never have chosen, the art crammed onto the walls, his handiwork evident in a headboard he'd crafted from a barn-door lintel and the cabana he was building around a hot tub in the back. I didn't have to fight him for control of the atmosphere.

We sat down to a lunch he'd made, exactly as we had on our second or third date, spaghetti in bowls and a good red wine, eaten at his small bar, this time with all that shared history, the tenderness and the rage, between us. ("Unhappily deceived," as Eve says to Adam, by a life that went so dramatically astray [10.917].) And our dog Jack, sniffing the floor for whatever might fall.

It wasn't a reconciliation. Call it the wild work of two people who can't sustain being in limbo much longer, but haven't quite formalized the changes they've wrought in their bond. Let us "strive / In offices of love," says Adam at last, relenting in his fury, to ease "each other's burden" (10.959–61). The truth is, the opposite of self-determining choice is plain old garden-variety ambivalence. "All I ever wanted was to see you smile," he said to me once, "and all you ever wanted was for me to see you cry, and know what that meant." You can choose to be heartbroken by such a remark, its sorry implication of two people who were destined, no matter how hard they tried, to misunderstand each other. Or you can choose never, no matter how frustrated or estranged you feel, to drive one another into extinction.

8

BARGAIN

THE UNIVERSE

In Paradise Lost, Death is the fearsome and insatiable child of Satan and his daughter Sin. The very word appears more than forty times in book 10 alone, as if "all conquering Death" (10.591) were ravenously chomping its way through the book like a demonic Pac-man. It's significant that the aftermath of one bad meal produces a range of alimentary distortions. The rebel angels, turned now to snakes, are condemned with perpetual hunger and thirst; they keep falling for the illusion that the fruit of hell, so like the one of Eden, will satisfy them, but their mouths fill up instead with "Soot and cinders" (573). The hounds of hell will lick and suck on "glutted offal" (633) till the coming of Christ. Sin is daily cannibalized by her own "odious offspring" (2.781)—the issue of Death—who slink back to the womb to "gnaw / [her] bowels" (2.799–800), while Satan promises her that in the new world he's about to create, she can binge to her heart's content, "fed and filled / Immeasurably" (2.843–44). Death simply "pine[s]" with "eternal famine" (597).

All of this reminds us that we are embodied creatures, even the heavenly ones. All of it is a terrible perversion of the good eating that happened at that long-ago luncheon for which Eve tempered the fruits and nuts and seeds of the garden, the one an archangel tucked into with "keen dispatch" (5.436). And so it dramatizes one of Milton's core philosophies: that food is a form of self-fashioning. We are what we eat, Milton would have believed as a seventeenth-century man schooled in that literal idea, the theory that the delicate balance of bodily condition and temperament, mood, behavior could be controlled—and so also disrupted—by what we consume. Our bodies, ourselves. Or to put it slightly differently, we are not just what we eat, but *how* we eat. Indiscriminate eating, eating without regard to the actual *identity* of what is being ingested—substance is subjectivity in this equation—wreaks havoc on us. The ultimate difference between the lunch Eve and Adam share with Raphael and the unhappy, voracious gobbling of Death and Sin lies less in how much they have than in their ability to respect, even recognize, what it is they're having.

This is no fanciful metaphor. Throughout his political writing, Milton repeatedly uses images of ugly consumption (gorging, gulping food down unchewed, vomiting, burping, and the like) to condemn the abuse of power and to accuse the lazy habit of not thinking independently. "Knowledge is as food," the archangel says to Adam (7.126). To know a thing well and thoroughly, to really understand it, we have to "concoct" it, a word that would have connoted for Milton both digestion and ripening. Judicious eating is thus synonymous with the kind of thoughtful judging and discerning that help us to make good choices. Maybe more, it's distinctly creative. Breaking something down to incorporate it, to make it a part of your bodily self, changes you, re-forms you slightly differently from what you just were.

It's important that Miltonic eating is philosophically connected to an ability to tolerate difference. Only when we allow the other into us (call it apple, call it controversial idea, call it dream you wake up from with your heart beating fast or person who arrives at your house with his noise-making tools and loud voice and habit of neglecting your moods), only when we can pause to consider a conundrum from all sides, only *then*, Milton would say, can we work through confusion or pain toward deeper understanding. It's no accident that the bloated constipation of Sin and Death—"crammed and gorged" they are, as God sneers to the Son (10.632)—is juxtaposed to delicate angelic excretion. Or that Adam and Eve have to eat bad fruit to regenerate their love. Eating the apple does mean loss—for one thing, they start aging the minute they swallow—but also a more inspired happiness. This is why, at the end of the epic, "fallen" Eve gets up from a dream she's had and tells Adam that whatever he knows, *she* knows, and why

Adam, at long last, shuts up and lets her have the last word: because they've worked their way at last to mutual respect. They've taken the risk of incorporation.

The way to the heart is actually the stomach.

I've been eating-disordered for most of my life. I haven't said that out loud so frankly in more than thirty years. Indulging and restricting, that's my particular bent. Let's say we're defined by the perpetual breaching of our boundaries by food. Some of us have relaxed, instinctive borders. I do not. I deploy restriction as control; it feels safe. Indulgence is release, a delicious letting-go of that iron grip I might feel I'm keeping, on—what, some notion of buoy in a wildly heaving sea? Experience is so desperately overwhelming. Food is *there*. It pleases and punishes in dependable alternation. It enlivens your senses, then it deadens them. It keeps us alive as we make our way toward dying. You can enjoy a meal with family and friends. You can always choose to eat alone. You can eat to celebrate, to wallow, to deny. You can eat because you've earned it, or because you deserve to feel wrong.

I've been to more than one meditation retreat where we were taught to eat mindfully through a single raisin. This is both maddening and ineffective. Milton's imagery makes more sense, if only I could live by it. All those ceaselessly chewing babes of Sin, the mouths of hell, maws of wolves, and "fangs of brutes" the poet associated with uncritical subservience to convention, with annihilation of the precious and legitimate separateness of all things. It isn't *temperance* that appeals to me, goodness no (Milton-as-fusty-Puritan has never rung true). It's *authenticity* that matters, residence in the intersubjective space of recognition, where we are ourselves, and where we love because we recognize—in the sense of allowing the separate humanity of—the other. That image of Eve mixing together "taste after taste" with "unsparing hand" (5.336, 344), because it underscores the capacity to hold contraries in balance, also seems liberated from fretting about limits, or authority, or showing off. She isn't completely undone by the fact of things, in themselves, abundant and delicious.

All this is hard-won, of course. I don't think I've ever fully felt it. Certainly never in romance. Maybe it won't surprise that my husband and I had problems with food in common, though it was never discussed. Actually, I'd harangue him about losing weight, and he'd resist. His problem was "portion control," he'd say, but I thought that obscured the weight of emotional muck below the surface. Classic projection on my part. Because knowing the muck hasn't cured me of using food to comfort or discipline myself. It's not like I haven't done the work of excavation on myself.

In his biography of Milton, Edward Phillips, having lived with his uncle as one of Milton's first students, gives us the tantalizing detail that the poet occasionally interrupted his routine of "hard Study, and spare Diet" in "the Society of some Young Sparks of his Acquaintance." Milton would "so far make bold with his Body," says the nephew, "as now and then to keep a Gawdy-day." A "gaudy" was an annual college festival, but it could suggest more mundane merriment. Some say we're only meant to imagine that Milton, every so often, tied one on with his pals. I like the idea of him somehow making a little bolder with his body. No one ever suggests a more debauched connotation than binge drinking, since Milton so clearly valued the ideal (also the gratification) of chaste sexuality, from some of his earliest writings through the later epic poems. But Milton *made up* that word, *debauchery*, after all. He knew the pull of the sensual. And it hardly needs stating that food and drink are on a continuum with more sexual transgressions. I don't mean that a bag of Cheetos is interchangeable with a sex romp. You can just have the one so easily.

More than our own eating is at stake in Milton's imaginary. He's also concerned with the fate of *being food*. Consider the elegy *Lycidas*, whose famed and digressive outburst aligns the pious reader with sheep being eaten up by corrupt, mercenary priests who act only "for their bellies' sake" (1.114). This means that satisfying your hunger doesn't affect only you. Someone else might get hurt.

HOLDING ONTO this skeleton of a marriage has everything to do with death. I'm fifty-six, fearing the loss of my mind: the women on my mother's side have a history of such disintegration. Some years ago, during a bad bout of headaches, I was diagnosed with something called white matter disease. There's no known correlation between these idiopathic spots on the brain and a condition like Alzheimer's, but I make it anyway. (I've been a hypochondriac since I was in fifth grade and thought I had yellow fever, studying the Philadelphia Quakers in school.) Every day, I notice changes to my physical being. Everything has thickened. Everything is dry. I'm so stiff in the mornings that I walk to the bathroom like a 1930s Frankenstein. My friends are starting to retire. One recently told me that his alternative to long-term health insurance would be a series of six-month cruises, with a doctor on board and all that available food. I have spirited imaginary conversations with younger people about the challenges of getting older. All of a sudden, it seems, I'm at the threshold of the ending, with no children, no immediate family within two thousand miles. I was counting on marriage to offset the terror of that inexorable turn.

And maybe, like Adam and Eve, who become mortal only in the moment of transgression, I didn't *really* start thinking about dying until the afternoon I left my husband in the hospital to face his guilt, went home to a future suddenly defined by unanticipated perils, and I understood that we were both, with harrowing abruptness, heading into old age alone. (Is it true that we never die in our own dreams, that body and psyche collaborate in protecting us from that irrevocable verge?) An idea of heaven would be comforting right now. Who wouldn't want to think that our passing might be eased by the promise of ecstatic eternity, that we'll be reunited with everyone we've ever lost? What a lovely consolation. Without it, we're alone in our Heideggerian dying, which is an utterly nonrelational event that cannot be shared, cannot be known, by another. I wish I could be less afraid of that.

But is it really death that scares the most, or the diminishment and adaptations of aging? Given my family history, dementia looms most menacingly. I used to take some comfort in the idea that by the time I'd lost my mind I wouldn't know it, but I understand that change is incremental and we can certainly be aware of ourselves in the very process of alteration. It's fragility we can't stand, atavistically speaking—our fundamental helplessness to be anything other than fleshly, mortal beings, subject to random variability and so vulnerable in a way we try very hard to defy. Impairments of mind and cognition have long been coded as more damaging to a concept of personhood than sensory or mobility ones, so I fully grasp, trained as I am to think in social, political terms about disabilities, that my fears are partly bound up with the "packaging" of conditions like Alzheimer's— how it's represented to us in the media, how it looks to us when we consider where the elderly in our culture typically end up. This isn't to minimize the very real effects of cognitive decline on families, on caregivers, on individuals themselves. Just to say that I have recourse to an attitude about the inevitable mind-body changes of aging that ought to lessen the perceived *threat* of it.

I know my husband wants to be around in my later years, to lift me on and off the commode; reassuring me of that is one way he's making amends in the present. And for now, I'm not saying no. He turned sixty last year, he's doing what he can to create some order in his life, like renting enormous dumpsters to haul away decades of detritus from a decrepit barn at the back of his property. (The barn is real, and too easy as a metaphor.) Heidegger has another concept, being-toward-death, that's pleasingly simple, and a little less stark than the lonely singularity of one's own death. If we work backward from that absolute final moment, how do we want to fashion our current experience? What can death teach of us of life? Being aware of death does not mean fearing it, or living defensively against it. Quite the opposite. Mindfulness of death, as the Buddhists also say, sharpens our lived experience. Being-toward-death means letting a deathbed perspective guide us toward greater authenticity. If we could *really* live knowing now what we'll know then, what would fall away—the petty insecurity, the jealousy and competitiveness? Wouldn't we stop the skirmishes we're waging in our heads, perpetually, the rehearsed slights and the surface-body comparisons and the territorial exclusions? It's easy to think we're holding on, as my husband has—at once literally but also with unconscious intensity—to important *stuff*, the raw material of something grander we imagine we can build, as soon as we have time, resources, some elusive wherewithal. It takes gumption to decide to throw it all away.

Overwhelmed by our chaotic emotions, beset by the certitude of our own inadequacy, we cling to externals: material belongings, alcohol, thrill-seeking, organizing systems, food. Food in particular is incredibly useful in establishing an apparatus of control. It's the one vice we can't live without, except that our abuse of it can hasten our dying.

Needing it means that we can manipulate ourselves, torque ourselves in wildly hurtful directions, through the misuse of it. We can pretend to the illusion of safeguarding our borders. It's ironic in a double-loop kind of way that Milton so graphically associates death with eating, to emphasize the dialectic of our human lives, determined by the reality of their endpoints. It depresses me to admit that, after so much *introspection*, I still sometimes eat like a demonic ghoul, cramming the empty spaces in myself with sugar and salt. Maybe it's worse that such pleasure is so secretive, infused with shame. Maybe it's worst that I punished my husband for embodying my own tortured relationship with food. The saddest of all is that we had childhood trauma in common, but we never figured out what that meant.

I often ask myself what I'll want to know about my life when I'm nearer to a natural death. For Heidegger that kind of reckoning did not involve confrontation with a supernatural bookkeeper. I'm not sure what we do with the knowledge that we've hurt people we love, deeply and terribly. With that sort of regret. Or with the ruts and grooves of trauma that are too often laid down early and (I sometimes worry) impossible to smooth. Trauma collapses time, so that any present moment can feel indistinguishable from a haunted past, inflecting the future with its grim immortality. Maybe we fold that perilous future back on itself by ceding the fight for control. If the future is defined not by a series of imaginary burdens that may never come to pass but by a death we contemplate with equanimity, as the end of a natural arc, does that not have a calming effect? So we apologize for the wrongs we've done. But maybe we also forgive. Surely being-toward-death involves laying down arms where the smaller betrayals of a life are concerned. To live more fully is to die more easefully, and to be awakened at the moment of dying is to amplify our gratitude for life.

I REMEMBER A MORNING when I was very young, maybe eleven, when my parents were out of town, and I woke up and put on *those* corduroy pants and *that* turtleneck shirt because they were the right color, now we would call it sea-foam green but it was something else then, in 1976, because I thought that would stave off the obscure dread prickling at my consciousness. We call this superstition. It is also magical thinking. Is it a form of religious belief? Freud writes throughout *The Future of an Illusion* that religion emerges as a defense against childhood helplessness, so, perhaps. I remember sitting at the breakfast table with the neighbor who was babysitting my sister and me, feeling too hot in my turtleneck and sure the world was about to open up beneath me, suck the whole house down.

I believe a panic attack is an intimation of death.

There's something about getting on the scale every morning that organizes the inchoate. Not just the hours of a day but identity itself can be structured according to elaborate arrangements of food, deals we strike with the woundedness of our being (if I eat this or that, I'll *feel* something), with the threat of disappearing, not *mattering* (if I weigh this or that, I'll *be* something). Relationships can be practically *reliant* on such bargains, as we maneuver the conditions of our love, trying so hard and always failing to guarantee outcomes. (*If only you would . . .*) In a foundations-of-mindfulness class, I learn that we cannot think our way out of disordered eating habits. The prefrontal cortex, site of our higher reasoning powers, is also developmentally the youngest part of the brain, and so the first to go off-line in situations that activate intense emotion. This is why we revert to old habits so readily when we're stressed and triggered, why "willpower" might be a coercive internalization of social rules and expectations and not a truly free expression of who we are. Insisting that all it takes to change is an ever-tighter grip on ourselves practically guarantees the chain reaction back to where we began. The Buddha himself counseled a middle way between sensual indulgence and asceticism. In Milton, all that aggressive devouring seems inevitable from figures locked in static battles of having or not, heaven and hell, strict right and essential wrong. If only the poem had shown us the meal Eve and Adam eat *after* they quit bargaining with each other and the universe for an end to their grief and finally make up. That's an aspect of the aftermath of transgression I'd really like to sit in on.

My husband and I had a terrible fight one night when he wanted to go to a friend's birthday party and my cat Linc had just died. I did not know that *she* would be there, but still I felt we were doomed. He could not understand basic sadness, it seemed to me; he recoiled from conversations he suspected would end in me letting him know how wrong he was. "You don't know how bad things are," I said as he stood awkwardly above where I was lying on the bed, pretending to read, and he should've said but didn't, *yes, I do*. I remember that he did not end up going to the party, but I was hardly comforted by that. He told me only after the fact, after he'd accepted my proposal of marriage and we were all those years in, that he didn't believe in monogamy, as if that explained anything—or maybe it explains everything so totally that no other question pertains.

While my therapist of that era was not-so-subtly chiding me for being unsympathetic to my husband's recent business frustrations, said husband was off enjoying himself somewhere. Greed abounding. I don't mean just the affair. I too was hoarding self-righteous misery with all the relish of illicit pleasure. No one in those years, I'm trying to say, was happy. Anyone who's suffered an eating disorder knows exactly what I'm talking about, how goodness sours when it's tinged with disgust. We were working so hard to stabilize ourselves— helpless, as Adam thinks (but how can this be, in Paradise?), against a feeling of radical dis-ease in our surroundings—by filling up what felt like gaping interior voids. *If only, if only*. Magical thinking is a cousin of catastrophizing. How relentlessly we manufactured our reasons and our justifying, convoluted mental efforts at sense that the Buddhists describe as drunken monkeys who keep you up all night.

I would like to inhabit, even momentarily, the sort of intentional life of which waking up to sunlight and green tea and quiet meditation actually forms a part. For all my refutation of design, I still long to be *solved*. The Buddhists themselves, the meditation plan notwithstanding, would call this "clinging." But what if the "consolation yet secure" that someone says we "carry hence" (12.620–21) could be grasped in the here-and-now, just by releasing our grip? Buddha-nature. Maybe that's a concept it pays the atheist to buy into. "Hence" means *from now on* and also *away from here*. Distances of time and space that collapse when we relinquish the promise of a revelatory insight. A therapist doing body work once said to me, when she touched spots on my back so tender I practically came off the table, that the eightfold path out of suffering begins in curiosity. "It is not the object we avoid," she said. "It's our relationship to it that we investigate." That's what this whole thing has been about: learning to live—and so also one day to die—fully in the length of a single inhale.

DID YOU KNOW that Eden is not synonymous with Paradise? Colloquially, the terms get used as if they refer to the same location, but Genesis 2 tells us otherwise: "the Lord God planted a garden eastward in Eden, and there he put the man whom he had formed." This is why Adam and Eve are brought to the gate of "Paradise, so late their happy seat," then make their way "Through Eden" and out of *Paradise Lost* (12.642, 649). I've always been intrigued by the slippage, one the exacting Milton likely would not have approved. Surely "Edenic" *means* utopian? (It's a crossword puzzle staple.) Yet technically Eden is just a neighborhood, and paradise the blissful garden. It's paradise that the archangel Michael tells Adam he carries "within" (587), and paradise Eve refers to when she assures Adam on the brink of expulsion that "with thee to go, / Is to stay here" (12.615–16).

Milton is credited with first using the word "space" to refer to the cosmos. The closest I've ever come to the feeling of religious dread is what happens when I contemplate space in that sense. Where are we, if space has no boundary, if it is nowhere? Where is "where" without some point of perspective? That enormity, the sheer incomprehensibility of it, fills me with a sensation I *think* is akin to dread in the religious sense, a feeling of one's tininess in the scheme of things. It's the concept of infinitude that gets Adam all squirrely with nerves, chattering to Eve about not having merited their happiness. He needs purpose, he needs limitation; he needs *her*, finally, to keep him grounded.

But what *is* ground? How do we place ourselves—how do we trust that solid plane beneath us, standing tall in mountain pose, in eagle, in tree—if we also sense the "Spaces incomprehensible" (20) around us, knowing "Earth" to be "a spot, a grain, / An atom" (8.17–18), in an ever-increasing infinitesimalness that threatens to obliterate us? These are Adam's words, as he strives to fathom the very workings of the cosmos, "studious thoughts abstruse" (40). And it's at this point in a long afternoon's discourse that Eve, "With lowliness majestic," rises to "[go] forth among her fruits and flowers, / To visit how they pros-pered" (42, 44–45), as if all that talk of incalculable distance compels her toward touch, to *tend*, back to earth as tactile substance.

Rita Dove says that "outer space is / inconceivably // intimate," but I'm terrified by it, by the vastness of ocean, the breathless dark of my worst mistakes, the inexorable advance of myself toward my own aging. The counterintuitive solution to fear is to let go. Maybe that's what magical thinking really means, not to ward off fear by the con-stant courting of whatever manifests it but to cede control entirely, to fly like aerialists toward absolute emptiness. I think of Eve, pull-ing her hand from Adam's as she sets out on a fateful, or maybe just famed, solitary journey toward a certain fruit. The cataclysm of hu-man history is about to unfold. But also so much less than that, really, in *Paradise Lost*, just an inelegant human tumbling-down from the heights of pretense, arrogance, and misunderstanding, ordinary and agonizing, between a husband and wife. In a matter of hours, epically speaking, they're reunited again.

Maybe it matters to be precise about where we think we are, but I'm struggling to decide. Maybe the concentric bands of space we in-habit together, ever-tighter areas of supposed perfection, could stand to have their edges roughed and blurred a bit. Maybe, like Adam and Eve, we ought to strive a little less to get things right, take our mean-dering steps, embrace the ambiguity, walk *through*, as Milton puts it. Maybe it's factually wrong but also exactly right to think of them still in some Edenic-as-paradisal space even after the transgression that's gotten them kicked out of the garden—because now they know they can endure the worst sort of loss anyone ever predicted for them.

I WANT TO ASK my husband, the builder, in what shadows his guilts and longings were lurking, because I never suspected a thing. I'm greedy for wisdom about the many ways in which we get this kind of coupling wrong, even though we seem compelled to keep doing it. Even now, at this very instant, I don't rule out, not categorically, the idea of doing it again, even though I doubt it would make sense. I know that cleaning out the barn is my husband's version of being-toward-death, his effort to dig out from under the weight of old suffering, to live more calmly in the now. I went over recently to look at a wicker shelf unit he thought might work in my three-season room, an addition he built a few years before he left. He'd been telling me, with some pride, about how he'd lessened the contents of the barn by a third or more. I expected light, air, broad pathways through neatly stacked building materials and labeled jars of nails and screws. To me the reality looked like evidence of a lifetime of mild hoarding. I had to wend my way around garbage cans full of scrap wood, coiled bales of wiring and fencing and plastic plumbing tubes, hand-me-down furniture from someone else's move, on floorboards rotting through, all of it dimly lit through windows grayed with grime. But he was smiling at me broadly. He wanted me to know.

There's a moment in *Lycidas* when the speaker, like the drowned subject of the poem also a youthful poet, worries over the pointlessness of it all. What's the point of trying so hard, he cries into the void, when some Fury can come along and "[slit] the thin spun life" with a pair of "shears" (75–76)? When the culmination of any life is the cessation of life? We're all afraid of spinning out in space alone, running out of air, in the terrifying silence. We're seeking ballast with every meal we eat, every rock we save from a walk on the beach, the books we read and then put on a shelf, the thoughts we cache and luxuriate in the rehearsal of. We need that weight. Because we're dangling over a verge, all of us, and we're doing our best—we can surely hope—to hold on.

9

UNHANDED

When I had been separated but still married for exactly three years, the fourth finger on my left hand rebelled against rings. I'd taken off my engagement ring and wedding band right after the separation, put them in a tin box that sits on my bedroom dresser, with a pink birthday candle I can't remember the significance of and a tiny silk rose, origins also obscure. To cover the strange bare spot on that hand, to give my thumb something to do again, I first bought a tourmaline ring from the Sundance catalog, a double row of multicolored stones set in brushed silver. For a year I didn't take it off, but when the skin underneath erupted in red, itchy bumps—reacting to moisture, maybe, or the sharp unevenness of the band—I bought a blue topaz. I'd read a novel about a murder that takes place in a blue topaz processing plant. I'd never seen topaz in blue, and I liked the swimming-pool coolness of it in its ornate setting. And when my skin under that ring, after another year of continuous wear, suddenly burst into itchy redness, I determined that my body, fed up with this parade of rings-that-weren't-*the*-ring, simply put the kibosh on the whole sordid performance.

Like other parts of my aging body, my hands are becoming my mother's hands—her long fingers, the visible veins, skin losing its elasticity. My husband's hands, older than mine, might be described as *beefy*. Thick, round hands with heels (odd bodily conflation), like the butt end of a baguette, or a newel post, or a baby's bald head. The nails are ragged. One pinky was broken in a hockey game, and now its segments do not line up.

I've seen him work with those hands. They suggest confidence.

He is clumsy, he will fall off a ladder because he is not paying attention. He's electrocuted himself, dislocated his shoulders, nailed parts of himself to planks of wood. His knees are shot. But his hands are always sure. I will not forget the feel of them around my waist, as if they fit there.

When he had surgery on one of his pinkies, he gave me the ring he wore on that finger for safekeeping. The only finger of mine it would not fall off of was my thumb. I kept it there while his hand healed, and then he gave me another to replace it because he wanted the first one back (themes of interchangeability return). This new one was an etched silver ring with a weak spot at the edge of one indentation. I had it soldered back together at least once, until the day it split for good and I knew that another repair was out of the question. We'd been separated a few years by then. This ring joined the other two in the little tin box.

I only recently realized, sitting in the audience at an academic conference, that I'm fixated on men's hands. I was scanning the panel for wedding rings, that glint of gold or silver signifying status.

WHEN THE DOG went missing and before he was found, I adopted a shelter cat, a Maine Coon mix I named Malcolm in honor of my mother's Scottish roots. Friends drove an hour through a glaringly sunny December day to bring him home to me, because I was driving around the neighborhood putting Lost Dog flyers in mailboxes. The cat spent the first few hours of his life on Hopeful Lane in the bathroom, blinking at me, and later that night curled up in bed as I nibbled, desperate about the lost dog in the wake of the absent husband, on a dinner of Xanax and pretzels. *We're going to be good friends,* I said to the green eyes contemplating me from a cloud of gray fur. *But not right now.* When Jack came back, a few days later, the two of them regarded each other from across the species divide and then turned to me as if neither could understand why I'd hidden a vital truth about the state of affairs in this world. *I leave you for five minutes . . . Wait—dog?*

The dog and cat exist in a weird space of sibling detente. The impish feline poltergeist spends his minimally awake hours pawing objects onto the floor, which prompts me to feed him if I'm around, and simply disappears things if I'm not, and agitates the dog to eruptions of growling and territoriality. One morning I came down to an avocado on the floor beneath the dining room table. The next day I found salt sprayed across the rug of the den, the kitty-shaped shaker on its back like an upended turtle. A few days later, pepper. I texted photos of this bizarre time-lapse guacamole event to my husband. Sometimes I look up from a book or my laptop to catch them nose-to-nose, Jack with his perennially hopeful wagging tail and Malcolm—who was recently sedated to have his matted hair shaved in a lion cut and so now resembles a 1980s metal rocker from behind—backing up into his shoulders like a tweener about to be kissed.

In the first days of nonstop crying, my husband suddenly gone, I worried that I was damaging my empathetic dog, who wouldn't stop licking my tears. I made theatrical animal noises, sometimes sitting on the floor, from inside a grief that tore through me with electrical heat. Jack's eyes are brown, but at even a short distance they look black, and round, and full of soul. Not really the latter. I know it's an evolutionary thing, that dogs have developed subtle movements in the muscles around their eyes—they can raise their eyebrows—responding to eye contact with the humans they've grown up around. I first realized that Jack was twitching his eyebrows that way, reacting to a human emotional atmosphere, the semester we lived in Paris and his dad (so to speak) was suffering the first signs of business collapse. We were standing on the Pont Neuf one gray afternoon, about to make a wish on a wishbone we'd dried for the purpose, with Jack in my husband's arms, eyebrows wiggling as he tried to figure out what was taking so long, what the buzz of discontentedness between us would mean for his future.

I'm projecting, of course.

But this brings me back to Jack getting lost, where this story began, and the ache I've felt to live so quintessentially myself, secure in the trust of all the good that's about to happen, in the manner of dogs, and all of Milton's natural world as he tells it in *Paradise Lost*, raucously alive and inherently capable of maneuvering through a complex environment. In the manner of Eve, who exercises the fullest potential of her human imagination without all this sedimented imposition of narrative on her experiences. Oh, "adventurous Eve" (9.921)! It is impossible to say what she knows of what lies ahead, as she prepares to garden alone, in the thickets of Paradise, lately the site of conjugal bliss but also marital woe, now threatened by an interloper with his own woundedness and pride, lurking in the shadows with designs on revenge. We know only what Milton writes of her, which is one bad apple, quickly consumed, followed by the recognition that we exist in relation to others, that we thrive only because of our others. Then a melancholy, though no less joyful, exit with Adam from so-called Paradise.

Alain de Botton tells us that religions are canny not just in appealing to our need for strong community, but also in acknowledging a baser truth that to some extent, in certain contexts, we really don't like each other at all. Religions use ritual, he explains, "to safely discharge what is vicious, destructive or nihilistic in our natures" (58). Ritual, de Botton says, mediates the self-interestedness that tugs us away from each other and gives us a structure through which to channel narcissism and arrive at fellowship. "Religions are wise," he goes on, "in not expecting us to deal with all of our emotions on our own" (61). Ritual is defined by its strictness: a set pattern of behavior, a calendar of execution, a prescribed space, the necessary accouterments, and the company of others. It's the *management* that counts, says de Botton. When we commemorate emotion in performing ritual's mechanisms, we're able to purge it; in the exhibiting of strong emotion, we are relieved.

I once accused my husband of not understanding irony. He said, "Is it the wagging tail?" We suffered a kind of clichéd dog-cat *men-are-from-wherever* discordancy. Nose-to-nose, recoiling. Here's what I'm getting at: when my husband was still recovering from heart surgery in the hospital, we took a walk down the hall toward a bank of windows overlooking a parking lot, highways, expanse of sky. It was July then, and I had the impression of knowing but not sensing heat, shimmery air on the other side of glass from the cool interior, a cognitive discrepancy of a sort that was soon to pervade my life. My husband clasped my hand to his sewn-up chest as we paced, up one side and down the other. *My love my love my love,* he said, as he often did, often had, but different somehow that day. *My love my love.* I had an inkling of, but of course could not comprehend, how terrified he was of dying. Staples through the bones of his sternum. It was hard to walk that way, slowly, my hand torqued upward and sideways to his heart. Feeling slightly irritated about that was my own way of disguising fear. He'd never intended to blow up our marriage. I believe that to be true. But that's what happens when you forget that love itself requires its rituals, and that our ideas about love do not help us translate the ferocity of our darknesses.

Touching is at the core of Milton's portrayal of rapprochement after more than one of his married couples' humdinger arguments. Skin to skin, that tactile remembrance of here and now, has the power to recall two people to the love of one another from the brink of epic violence. For a long time it bothered me that my husband drove with one hand ever on my thigh, that he couldn't walk the dog without also holding my hand, that he needed to be touching while we sat and watched TV. By the time it bothered me less, that *need* of his, that fear of losing the tether, and I'd realized the potency of a simple touch in the midst of anger, we were already angry more than we loved, swept along by the righteous stories we were orating about the myriad wrongs the other had committed. By the time our hopeful couples therapist kept inviting us to turn to each other and take the other's hand, we were downright insatiable ghosts, demanding a satisfaction—by which I mean pleasure, but also recompense— that the other could never provide. For six months after we split, I craved his hands, his mouth, his body anywhere on my body. Later there were therapy sessions in which I lost my own body entirely, so thorough was the raging strain of sadness, and I could not tolerate his touch.

As our singularly dexterous appendage, hands have been symbolically linked to ideas of personhood for a very long time. The Latin root *manus*, meaning "hand," shows up in all sorts of words denoting specifically human forms of power and control, including "command," "manipulate," "maneuver," and "manufacture." Ancient Greek philosophers like Aristotle and Galen refer to hands as signs of humanity's special relationship with God, the corporeal extension of soul. Think of that iconic detail from the Sistine ceiling where Adam and God stretch their arms toward each other, fingertips nearly but not quite touching—the bodily likeness signifying another, more immaterial correspondence. When Milton famously ascribed his political writing of the 1640s and 1650s to his left hand, he wasn't just invoking a dichotomy of parts—since the Latin *sinistra*, "left," contains "sinister"— or reminding us of the actual physical process of composition with pen and ink; he also made the hand a direct extension of mind and imagination: a synecdoche we find in expressions like *all hands on deck* or that devilish nonsense about *idle hands*. Representations of and references to hands connote all manner of social and political abstractions, from justice to protest to mercy.

So it makes sense that we use our hands, touch with our hands, to signal tenderness and solidarity, in times of anguish and in moments of prayer, forming a tactile chain of connection. Touching has documented therapeutic benefits, too, from lowering blood pressure, heart rate, and anxiety to stimulating growth and the healing of wounds. Bonds between babies and their earliest caregivers happen at the threshold of skin, with the lightest of touches integral to forming attachments. The process of "gentling," or regular manual handling, can decrease the process of aging in certain animals, and in one renowned primate study, rhesus monkeys chose to cuddle with a fabric-covered wire "mother" even in the absence of food. Touch is our most archaic sense, given our origins in the womb, in the memory we carry of two bodies in the closest possible proximity.

To come into contact this way, skin-to-skin, activates the physical and symbolic edge of ourselves—the dynamic, porous organ of skin that regulates our interactions with the world. We think of touch as having to do with connection, but doesn't it inevitably entail an encounter with difference? Even to touch oneself is to put two separate entities, with differing intensities and forms of feeling, into communication. The further we get from our own boundaries, the greater the potential for an ethical dimension in the realm of physical contact; in bridging the border between, touch requires that that we take something of the other into ourselves—literally, in skin cells that transfer from one body to another, and figuratively, in the creation of contiguity, in a gesture of acceptance and willingness. This is why the image of hands holding hands has been used in so many corporate and organizational logos, to assure us of the promise of cooperation. Holding hands suggests a lateral bond, one that, in acknowledging likeness-in-difference, figuring reciprocity, disrupts hierarchy. Hands held form a new totality, a hybrid whole comprised of identifiable—because they never get subsumed or overpowered—individual parts.

Paradise Lost utilizes hand imagery in just this fashion, if also in recognizable dichotomies. Forms of *hand* appear more than a hundred times in the epic, most often over the course of Raphael's account of the war between Satan's faction and the Son's, where hands are associated with the dirty business of transgression as well as the virtuous reestablishment of order. Hands are far from neutral body parts in all of this. To the contrary, they register significant ideological commitments: to relationships, to political groups, to various kinds of work, even to oneself.

So Adam and Eve "talk hand in hand" in sweet, hopeful times (4.689), and "Handed they [go]" to their nuptial pleasures (739). When Eve takes her leave of him, heading off to garden alone, "from her husband's hand her hand / Soft she withdrew" (9.385–86). That syntax of these last lines is important, first drawing out the drama after "from," making us wait, in terrible realization of what's on the brink, for the grammar to resolve; then piling up *husband's hand her hand*, making "hand" seem both verb and noun, moving in two directions; and finally pausing, creating an awful tension, before "withdrew," so that we might wonder if she will or won't, maybe wishing she would go one way or the other. Later, when Eve returns to Adam after eating the apple, her cheeks "flushing" with the news of it (9.887), she holds "in her hand" a bough from that fateful tree (850), and when he realizes what she's done, the garland Adam has been weaving for her drops "from his slack hand" to the ground (892). By the end of the poem, with providence as guide and Eden not a place but a word for reconciliation, something they carry within as a means of choosing what comes next, they're hand in hand again. Even when they're being ushered out of paradise, it's their hands "the hastening angel caught" (12.637).

In Milton's final poem, the closet-drama *Samson Agonistes* (written in imitation of ancient Greek tragedy but never intended for live performance), touching takes on an even more explicit ethical dimension. If traditional dating is to be respected, *Samson* was composed in the late 1660s—after Milton had been briefly in hiding and then imprisoned for his advocacy of regicide, but while the shifting policies and allegiances of the restored monarchy forced him into delicate social and political negotiations to keep himself safe. The drama opens with the blind hero Samson, the Israelite judge, imprisoned by the Philistines and doubting his interpretation of God's "motions" within him; it ends with him bringing a roof down "upon the heads" of idolatrous Philistine nobility, gathered for a feast to celebrate their defeat of Samson, from whose "hands" they believe themselves to be delivered. Many have detected an autobiographical tone of bitter, war-weary frustration, even a kind of revenge fantasy, in that arc. In Samson's supplicating Philistine wife, Dalila, meanwhile, it's easy to imagine an allusion—or a retroactive sneer—at that infamous Mary Powell, whose Royalist family had clashed with Milton's republican sympathies decades before.

There hasn't been a semester of teaching Milton when I don't run out of time and fail to do justice to this dense and intriguing text, and I end up compressing it to one essential point: the foregrounding of competing perspectives. *Samson* proceeds in dialogue—there is no stage direction—so that any action, in the immediate or witnessed, remembered, and retold, is subject to the bias of the speaker. Ambiguity in this sequence is inevitable. We are repeatedly invited to consider that a fundamental significance of events cannot be proven—or that they do not have a single meaning at all, even ones purportedly intended by a god. As the text proceeds, and characters with differing perceptions of events assert their respective realities, explanatory certainty becomes more and more elusive—until, at the climax, the meaning of Samson's violent last act, reported to his father Manoa thirdhand by a Messenger, recedes in a haze of indeterminacy. Samson had "stood, *as* one who prayed, / *Or* some great matter in his mind revolved" (1637–38; my italics). But what do we glean from that description? It matters that while the existence of Samson's god is not at issue, his interpretation of their relationship is acutely precarious.

How can we feel sure that any decision, any action, is the *right* one, the sanctioned one, the one to recompense a whole string of questionable choices, with no certifiable guarantee?

It's important too that Milton fabricates a marriage at the core of all this. (Samson and Dalila are not husband and wife in the scriptural Judges, where the woman is a notorious seductress.) Making them a married couple raises the stakes of their entire interaction. Dalila comes to the prison to plead with Samson to forgive her for revealing his secret—the secret of where his strength is stored—to her people. Or if not to pardon, at least to acknowledge how much pressure she was under to play the mole, "solicited, commanded, threatened, [and] urged" (852) by Philistine priests and magistrates to betray her husband. While the poem cleverly, and carefully, uses verbal echoes to create a resonance between these seemingly obvious enemies, Samson remains rigidly dogmatic throughout their conversation, growling defensively about lost honor and shame.

It's Dalila who makes the critical ethical move, asking permission to "approach at least, and touch thy hand" (951). That yearning to touch is far from inconsequential in this tale of battling sides, where the wounded Nazarite husband cannot cease repudiating his penitent Philistine wife, perhaps especially because Samson has been blinded by Dalila's people. Both bodies are compromised: not in any real or essential way, but because each is readily available to interpretation as such by the opposing group—Samson's blindness, just like Milton's, insulted as proof of his weakness, Dalila's gender and ethnicity easy targets of scathing insult. The ability to set aside the judgments of others, to ignore the ideological norms of one's own tribe, to reach out to make intimate physical contact with similarity in a world of difference—maybe that's the truest definition of love. Inclusivity demands not sameness but the acceptance of otherness. Dalila's touch has such radical symbolic potential.

There's something striking and brilliant about a poet like Milton, at the end of a long career, after a series of bloody civil wars, in the midst of political upheaval, imagining that quiet moment of hoped-for caress, writing that sorrowful request: *Let me approach at least . . .* It's one more in a series of failed attempts to calm Samson's anger, an appeal to his past affections for her—it is, of course, all that—but it's also a sideways deke that slices through the volume of ineffectual words with a more potent possibility. That Samson reacts most aggressively to the threat of Dalila's touch, more than to anything she says—that he refuses the feel of her hand, specifically—does not invalidate her effort. To the contrary, it confirms Samson's sense of vulnerability. The intensity of his continued attachment.

If it weren't for the logic of teaching a writer's material more or less in order, I might begin a class with this text, to lay down patterns of inscrutability and bewilderment we could trace the antecedents of in earlier work. All the urgent talking of *Samson Agonistes* measures its worry. How do we keep the faith when all evidence says we're forsaken? Why carry on at all when circumstances are so dire? Can we ever trust again the ones who've betrayed us? How to make sense of a world so full of signs that refuse to reveal their meaning? Or worse— what do we do if there are no signs at all, only other people, with their maddening, persistent, alternative opinions? Do we rally our righteous anger and bring the house, literally, down? Or should we set past treacheries aside, and accept someone's hand?

THE MAN WHO taught me Milton taught me a single thing about Keats. We were in a metaphysical poetry class, talking about the lyrical *you,* and how convincingly certain poems convey the presence of the one being addressed. John Donne does this brilliantly in "The Flea," where the woman the speaker is cajoling toward sex through the device of the flea apparently *acts* in the blank space between stanzas—squashing the flea itself—so that the poem has to stay in motion, readjust its intentions, in response to her.

But it's Keats's "This Living Hand," according to my teacher, that engages *you* with the most thrilling immediacy, invoking, simultaneously, someone unnamed in the poem, and the reader, and maybe Keats's betrothed, Fanny Brawne, or his friend Leigh Hunt, appealed to for comfort as the poet lay dying. The identity of *you* doesn't really matter, finally, but the strikingly direct quality of the poem's *use* of the word, its creation of a sense of dynamic, certainly does. *You* doesn't actually appear until the poem's final line, in a sudden switch from the more informal "thy" and "thou," and it's because of that change in register that the poem seems, in its last moment, to grab hold of us as we read, reaching out in nearly a corporeal way. It's hard not to feel startled, almost as if someone has burst into the room, intruding on a private experience. *Here,* writes Keats, many years after Milton, and just before he died, *this living hand, I hold it towards you.*

This living hand, stretched toward some beloved other, in pain or hopefulness or dread. When my husband and I got married, in the town where we live, we did not exchange rings. He had some reason for not wanting, or being able, to have one on the fourth finger of his left hand, a reason I do not remember. I was already wearing the silver band he'd given me the week before, at a ceremony we held with family and friends in France. Instead we followed, more or less exactly, a hand-binding ritual I'd discovered online. We were trying to craft a wedding outside of tradition, more consistent with our own beliefs and involving our closest relationships. Our officiant, one of my husband's brothers who'd gotten ordained for seventy-five dollars by the Universal Life Church, wrapped a MacKenzie tartan ribbon, my mother's family plaid, around our hands. We made promises to each other, cribbed from the online description. I still have the slip of paper on which I wrote our separate parts of these declarations— promises of laughter, honesty, dependability, compassion, warmth— and the ribbon, folded inside a beaded clutch purse that belonged to my grandmother.

The handfasting ritual seemed like a perfect way to structure our ceremony nonreligiously, to incorporate something of our respective Scottish and Irish heritages, to nod to the quiet receptivity of mindfulness and even my husband's Druidic proclivities. I liked knowing it had both ancient origins and current popularity—I found that reassuring somehow, the participation in something *known* even as we spun it in our private direction. We had the ceremony in a big field, with all our guests in a circle around us, holding candles that were lit, one by one from person to person, beginning with my mother and ending with one of his sisters, as the closing act. Everything we did was meant to carry some weight like that, to avoid contrivance and to symbolize the joining of our selves, our families, our lives. I don't regret any part of it, even the crashers who hitched themselves to the Canadian contingent or the friend who got drunk and drowned out my father's toast with his obnoxious guffawing. It was all part of an experience I was determined to relish, and did, as one of the happiest days of my life.

It was only later, at the start of fall, that I began to feel overwhelmed by the enormity of it. *A crisis to the system,* my mother once called marriage, that reorganizes us completely. When we were first together, my husband and I, we never allowed arguments to last overnight, as horrendous an evening as that sometimes made for, and we had learned from a therapist we once saw that some kind of touch—a hand on an arm, fingers entwined, even just two knees pressed slightly against one another as you sit defensively on a couch—could help to defuse the most potent of arguments. But then, maybe you come down in the morning, or home from work, to a note handwritten on several sheets of scratch paper, waiting for you on the kitchen counter, letting you know that *love might not be enough,* and your world tilts and keens and blurs out of focus. The irony is, we should have let each other go then, only three years in, though we managed to patch ourselves up. Because something had broken that year, and I felt the cracks, the grit against my palms, for a long time after.

We had made "tying the knot" literal in our handfasting ritual, and too soon the tail ends of that blasted ribbon were flapping about in the winds of misunderstanding. He was right to imply that love wasn't enough, because we also craved each other's approval, and tolerance, a kind of blanket approbation for however we might conduct ourselves. I don't mean that we didn't try hard to communicate with each other, to cede space to the other's habits and desires, but the best selves we wanted to be got so complicated by the pantomime of unconscious *stuff* we couldn't accurately identify. Does it make any kind of sense to think that atheism, in depriving us of figures of perfection like angels or saints, funnels our need to worship and adore into romantic love? Or do we owe our troubles to the legacy of Protestant companionate marriage, the early modern ideal of two people joined as *friends* as much as lovers—which, in seeming to make marriage a convenient and effective partnership, also conspires to make us believe that we can, and should, have all our needs satisfied by one person?

Unless that one person is ourselves, I suppose. I sometimes wish I could wear my engagement ring again without raising eyebrows and inviting critique. It's a tension set diamond (a small one) in a silver band. In a tension setting, the gem is held in suspension simply by the pressure of the metal. A jeweler will tell you that though tension rings look fragile, as if the gem is precariously floating and risks falling out because there's no mechanical support, they are in fact extremely durable. I'd never seen such a setting before, and beyond the aesthetics of its smooth lines, without prongs to hold the jewel, I appreciated the symbolism of it. All of these terms—*tension, suspension, support*—so obviously pertain to the relationship whose endurance the circular ring is meant to represent, as the manifestation of a delicate love two people are responsible for cradling between them. I'd like the idea of sporting my own tension-held self-love on my hand if it weren't so trendy for single women to wear self-commitment rings and so obviously acquiescent to marriage as the still-dominant ideal of social worth. Anyway, I'd be forever explaining myself if I put my engagement band back on. And is it totally honest to say it's just a pretty ring? What overdetermined emotional baubles these are.

Instead I've got the tourmaline on that finger again. It's bulky where the tension set is sleek and clean, but it has nothing to do with conventional weddings, and I tell anyone who asks that I bought it for myself.

MAYBE SAMSON IS right, and we're best served by leaning into the satisfactions of a justified fury, as Samson leans against a pillar of the Philistine temple, eyes closed tight, just before the roof comes down. I suppose I admire his adamant refusal to relent. How to keep the faith in the wake of extreme betrayal. Don't think I don't know this has dragged on a while (*my love my love*), up one corridor, down the other. When I talk to my therapist these days about my indecision and the boundaries I'm ineptly maintaining, the anger and crushing disappointment that interactions with my husband can still provoke and the presence in my life of a love I don't want to forego, she gets a certain look on her face. She's never instructed me to finalize a divorce, only to be better at protecting myself from an impulse to help, to shield, to hold us in some sort of *place* with each other. It's also Dalila that I admire, after all, for her generosity, her ironic forthrightness ("In argument with men a woman ever / Goes by the worse," she says, hilariously, "whatever be her cause" [903–4]). And Eve, of course, whose self-reliance and "answering looks / Of sympathy and love" have captivated my longing to be easier with myself, *in* myself, for more than half my life. They have no trouble sticking up for themselves, Dalila and Eve, but they don't shy away from genuine contrition, either, when it's called for.

The lesson I take from these marriages, in which wives are emotionally supple and husbands variously outraged, vengeful, fawning, and full of enthusiastic plans for the future, is that we never know if someone will take our hand, and we'll never pin down a formula for getting it right even if they do. That's the gamble of this life (*my love*). Isn't it odd to think that a seventeenth-century man like Milton would have been less terrified by divorce than I? *Don't go!* I'd like to say to Eve, as she's pulling her hand away from Adam's and about to enter what will amount to the worst phase of her Edenic existence. But also, to both of them, husband and wife, *it's about time.* Get the hell out of Dodge. Nurture your independence, and test, truly test, the unknown. Lateral reciprocity: that's what it means to be hand in hand. Aloneness-in-unity. The capacity to be oneself in the face of opposition, and to hold out love toward the aggravation of disparity. "It is not for me to impeach your truth," my husband emailed to me recently, in his quirkily formal way, "even if mine is different." I can't decide if that's impossibly sad, too little too late, or beside the point, since in seeming to acknowledge the validity of another point of view, it merely redraws the barrier between us.

My whole life, I've been searching for meaning. The poet Bill Matthews once remarked, in his dust-moted uptown flat, that I was obsessed with knowing. (I'd have gotten kicked out of Eden for that.) I understand that the inclination, call it a desperation, to contain our experiences in the comforts of narrative explanation embroils us in a false sense of security and control over the throes of existence. The Buddha would tell me to lay down the "second arrow" of my mental machinations. We only worsen our suffering when we forget to be with what is.

I turn again toward the possibility of equanimity. Take little Jack, now twelve, who had surgery last week—a full seven masses, all benign, removed from just under his skin. It was a two-hour procedure, and I carried him into the house that day like a patchwork quilt of shaved squares and ragged incisions. But he didn't require coddling. He was ravenous, ate four small meals throughout the afternoon with his usual gusto. He wriggled with excitement when my husband came to visit, then settled himself contentedly as my husband and I stood in the driveway and talked across each other in a way I've come to mourn, or dread, as inescapably depleting (lines I love from Marilyn Nelson Waniek's *Magnificat* floating through my head: "look what faith got me: / A weird, almost non-relationship / with an inscrutable, cantankerous old hermit"). Jack didn't care. The embodiment of pure presence wouldn't squander a patch of grass bathed in late-summer sun. And that evening, as we walked, Jack snuffling along the ground for a good place to pee, it occurred to me that he was hardly feeling sorry for himself, for his ordeal of the morning—thinking *fragile* or *I'll take to my bed* or needing sympathy or notice. He'd been through something, alright; he bristled with stitches and he was up and down all that night, unable to get comfortable enough to stay asleep. But he was not metaphysically suffering. There was pain. There was the promise of joy.

So here's what I know, even if I can't guarantee I'll ever do more than aspire to it. We want what we want, be it understanding or respect or good conversation or hope, and we mustn't confuse such needs with weakness or spite. But we can also live ourselves right *here*, nurture the refuge within. Whatever the traumas we've endured, however we've been wronged, whomever we've hurt—the most important moment is this moment, we can set the treacheries aside, refuse resignation, remember to care. No matter our differences, my friends (*my love*)—you, me, let's embark on what's next, no delay. That's where this all began, at the end of a tale of great loss, Eve calling to Adam as they stride off together, hand in hand (nose to nose, call it what you will). You, me, the dog, the cat, however you configure your love. Feet on the earthly ground. Into the wild beyond.

DEDICATIONS

I HAVE TRIED and failed to find words sufficient to express gratitude to those whose love sustains me in this life, more than they could ever fathom—my mother, Beth MacKenzie (who gave me Bion and so much more), my sister and confidante Leah E. Mintz, my sister and pandemic compatriot Alexis Mintz (I am in awe of these brilliant, independent, amazing women), and my stepfather, Steve Dubinett (a man of staggering generosity). This book is better for the astute suggestions of friends who read complete drafts—Chad Davidson, Jay Rogoff, Matt Roth, Martha Wiseman—and the meticulous input of Katie Gougelet, former editor at *Sonora Review*. Similar thanks to Sylvie Bertrand and Christopher X. Shade at *Cagibi*, and Kwame Dawes and Ashley Strosnider at *Prairie Schooner*, for guiding me toward better prose, and to James Long for his endorsement, and giving me a home at LSU Press.

Decades of heads-bent, shoulder-to-shoulder conversation with Susan Walzer are threaded through these pages, Miltonic confabulation at its best; I've absorbed so much of her wisdom that some of my words are likely hers. To Ann S. Biasetti, who entered my life when I needed to learn—or remember—the meaning of resilience, I owe such an enormous debt. For a long time Greg Fraser helped me to grow up, and now he is easing my fears of middle age. To my friend Melora Wolff, the essayist I wish I could write just like; to Mason Stokes and John Peabody, who have fed me with innumerable lovely meals and shop-talks about genre, form, and process; to David Fraser, who once sent me a library microfilm card of *Paradise Lost;* to Sal Peralta, who shared his remarkable story with me; to Ralph Savarese, who read my manuscript and leads by example; and to Barbara Black, who always asked, and whose enthusiasm was a buoy she may not have known she was tossing me—to these cherished friends, thank you. I'm grateful to Linda Simon, for always having a ready list of titles, and being herself, and knowing me; to Beau Breslin, for coffee and commiseration about the unhappy surprises of the publishing world; and to Tom Couser, collaborator of many years, who has extended to me so much more support than I could have imagined meriting. Lisa Johnson offered sage advice about projects like this. Matthew Hockenos (here's to the return of taco Tuesdays) sets the bar for productivity.

I thank my Convivio compatriots—Leslie Carlisle, Bob Haeberlin, Eric Smith, Mary Moore, Ellen Doré Watson, Barbara Ras, Ed and Amanda Wilson, Brian Hawkins, Anne Barnhart, Roger Carlisle, Craig Schroer, John Poch, Dionne Breymer, Chris Rolka, Jeff Thompson—for listening; this book took shape over several summers within their welcoming audience. I have had the privilege of extraordinary colleagues at Skidmore and thank my department for valuing work that presses the edges of category. Ben Bogin, Sonya Chung, and Brad Onishi read the very first chapters of this project, and helped me to discover what was at stake. In Milton classes and nonfiction workshops, I've worked with students whose intelligence, maturity, and creative talents have been a source of enormous inspiration—too many to name here, but especially Brian Allen, Sophie Dodd, Eliza Dumais, Dyani Johns, Helen Kirk, Nell Mittelstead, Kellina Moore, Jake Musich, Emily Robinson, Alexis Traussi, and the memoirists of Advanced Projects 2019. Special thanks to Catherine Golden and Michael Marx, who fetched the Maine Coon cat who figures here. To the men who rescued Jack—David Mattison and my neighbor Bob Schretzlmeir—and to Stacey Mattison, eternal gratitude for bringing the intrepid traveler home. *Love Affair* would never have happened without Jack.

Because this book loops its way through a few iterations of my writing and scholarly life, from creative work to Milton to mindfulness and back again, I acknowledge here many people who inform my sense of well-being—of being someone at all—including Jim and Lois Mintz, Amanda and Lauren Mintz, Wes Heartfield, Barbara Fraser, Milada Fraser, John Anzalone, Rebecca Whitehead, Joel Brown,

Beth Gershuny, Jo Fax, Gail Haines, Ashley Cross, Chris McGowan, Joanna Swyers, Erik Germani, Tracy Volz, Eric Spaeth, George Janku, Jennifer Delton, Chris Gabbard, and Sarah Goodwin. Finally, to the person who lived much of this story with me, Michael Belanger, who has never begrudged me the working-through of a story he tells in his own way, heartfelt appreciation for what we've built, in so many senses of that word.

WORKS CITED

Bion, W. R. *A Memoir of the Future*. London: Karnac, 1991.

Bishop, Elizabeth. "One Art." In *The Complete Poems*. New York: Farrar, Straus and Giroux, 1990.

Dalai Lama. *The Art of Happiness*. With Howard C. Cutler. New York: Riverhead, 1998.

Danquah, Meri Nana-Ama. *Willow Weep for Me: A Black Woman's Journey through Depression*. New York: Ballantine, 1998.

de Botton, Alain. *Religion for Atheists*. London: Penguin, 2012.

Dickinson, Emily. "Parting." In *The Complete Poems of Emily Dickinson*, edited by Thomas H. Johnson. Boston: Back Bay, 1976.

Dove, Rita. "Anti-Father." In *Selected Poems*. New York: Vintage, 1993.

Freud, Sigmund. *Civilization and Its Discontents*. Translated and edited by James Strachey. New York: Norton, 1961.

——. *The Future of an Illusion*. Translated by W. D. Robson-Scott. Revised and edited by James Strachey. New York: Anchor, 1964.

Goldbarth, Albert. *Dark Waves and Light Matter: Essays*. Athens: University of Georgia Press, 1999.

Hemingway, Ernest. "A Clean Well-Lighted Place." https://www.wlps.org/view/2546.pdf.

——. *The Garden of Eden*. New York: Scribner, 1986.

——. *A Moveable Feast*. New York: Scribner, 2010.

——. *The Sun Also Rises*. New York: Scribner, 1956.

Keats, John. "This living hand, now warm and capable." https://www.poetryfoundation.org/poems/50375/this-living-hand-now-warm-and-capable.

Larkin, Philip. "Church Going." In *Collected Poems*, edited by Anthony Thwaite. New York: Farrar, Straus and Giroux, 1989.

Lowell, Robert. *The Letters of Robert Lowell*. New York: Macmillan, 2007.

Mairs, Nancy. "Into the Wider World." In *Waist-High in the World*, 190–209. Boston: Beacon Press, 1996.

Milton, John. *Areopagitica, Eikonoklastes, The Doctrine and Discipline of Divorce, Lycidas,* "Of Education," *Second Defense of the English People,* Sonnet 19. In *The Complete Poetry and Essential Prose of John Milton,* edited by William Kerrigan, John Rumrich, and Stephen M. Fallon. New York: Modern Library, 2007.

———. *Commonplace Book.* In *Complete Prose Works of John Milton,* vol. 1. New Haven, CT: Yale University Press, 1953.

———. *Milton's Familiar Letters.* London: Wentworth, 2019.

———. *Paradise Lost.* Edited by Alistair Fowler. London: Longman, 1991.

———. *Samson Agonistes.* In *Complete Shorter Poems,* edited by John Carey. London: Longman, 1990.

Morrison, Toni. *Sula.* New York: Vintage, 2004.

Pascal, Blaise. *Pascal's Pensées: The Misery of Man without God.* CreateSpace Publishing Platform, 2010.

Phillips, John. *The Life of Mr. John Milton.* In *The Early Lives of Milton,* edited by Helen Darbishire, 17–34. London: Constable, 1932,

Rilke, Rainer Maria. *Letters to a Young Poet.* Translated by Stephen Mitchell. New York: Vintage, 1986.

Szymborska, Wislawa. "On the Banks of the River Styx." In *View with a Grain of Sand: Selected Poems.* New York: Harcourt Brace, 1993.

Tokarczuk, Olga. *Drive Your Plow over the Bones of the Dead.* Translated by Antonia Lloyd-Jones. London: Fitzcarraldo Editions, 2019.

Trethewey, Natasha. "Gathering." In *Monument: Poems New and Selected.* Boston: Houghton Mifflin Harcourt, 2018.

Trungpa, Chögyam. *Mindfulness in Action.* Boulder, CO: Shambhala, 2016.

Van Clief-Stefanon, Lyrae. "Tandem." In *Open Interval.* Pittsburgh, PA: University of Pittsburgh Press, 2009.

Walsh, John. "Being Ernest Hemingway: John Walsh Unravels the Mystery behind Hemingway's Suicide." *Independent,* 11 June 2011. https://www.inde pendent.co.uk/news/people/profiles/being-ernest-john-walsh-unravels-the-mystery-behind-hemingways-suicide-2294619.html.

Waniek, Marilyn Nelson. "The War of the Heart." In *Magnificat.* Baton Rouge: LSU Press, 1994.

CPSIA information can be obtained
at www.ICGtesting.com
Printed in the USA
LVHW032209070722
722962LV00003B/417